THE THEORY OF PROPORTION IN ARCHITECTURE

P. H. SCHOLFIELD

THE THEORY OF PROPORTION IN ARCHITECTURE

CAMBRIDGE: AT THE UNIVERSITY PRESS

MCMLVIII

CAMBRIDGE UNIVERSITY PRESS
Cambridge, New York, Melbourne, Madrid, Cape Town,
Singapore, São Paulo, Delhi, Tokyo, Mexico City

Cambridge University Press
The Edinburgh Building, Cambridge CB2 8RU, UK

Published in the United States of America by Cambridge University Press, New York

www.cambridge.org
Information on this title: www.cambridge.org/9780521243155

First published 1958
First paperback edition 2011

A catalogue record for this publication is available from the British Library

ISBN 978-0-521-24315-5 Paperback

FOREWORD

The contribution to the subject of visual proportion in architecture which Mr Scholfield makes in this book is both timely and important. He deals comprehensively with the history of the theory of proportion from antiquity up to the present time, with the sequence of systems— arithmetical and geometrical, commensurable and incommensurable— that have been elaborated and employed in Classic, Renaissance, Revivalist and contemporary architecture; and he formulates a theory in which the apparent contradictions of the major practical systems are convincingly reconciled. He also disposes effectively of the contentions of those theoretic anarchists who would in all circumstances deny the validity and reject the discipline of any consistent scheme of linear or spatial ratios.

In the section devoted to Vitruvius' observations on architectural proportion he suggests interpretations of the terminology used by Vitruvius that have the virtue of making it intelligible and reasonable. This in itself is no small achievement. His critical examination of Renaissance theory, its limitations, obsessions and illusions, and the causes and compensations of its collapse, is equally penetrating and significant. In discussing the consequences of that collapse, the reestablishment of the theory of architectural proportion on broader and more solid foundations and its further development in our own time, he draws on a wide range of first sources. His conclusions are reached by the exercise of an acute perception and an independent judgment that make the whole study a work of the highest interest and value.

To have been asked by the author to write a Foreword to a treatise of such quality is an honour which I greatly appreciate.

LIONEL B. BUDDEN

CONTENTS

CONTENTS

LIST OF ILLUSTRATIONS

PREFACE

In its original form this book was written as a thesis for the Degree
of M.A. at Liverpool University. I am deeply indebted to the late
Professor Budden, who not only contributed the Foreword, but without whose unfailing kindness and encouragement the work would never
have been carried out. I wish to thank Professor F. W. Walbank for
reading the chapter on Vitruvius, and making a number of helpful
suggestions. My debt to previous writers on the subject of architectural
proportion will, I think, be obvious from the book itself.

Finally, I am grateful to the Bibliothèque Nationale, Paris, for
permission to use plate 7, and to the following publishers for allowing
me to quote and make use of illustrations: Benno Schwabe and Co.,
Basle (plate 13, from Heinrich Wölfflin's *Kleine Schriften*); Ullstein
Aktiengesellschaft, Bauwelt Verlag, Berlin (plate 14, from Professor
Neufert's *Bauentwurfslehre*); Messrs Constable and Co., Ltd. (plates 15
and 16, from Sir Theodore Cook's *Curves of Life*); Oxford University
Press and Princeton University Press (quotation from Hermann Weyl's
Symmetry).

P. H. S.

April 1957

CHAPTER I

INTRODUCTION

There exists today a growing interest in the problem of proportion in architecture. We know from their writings that architects of the Renaissance applied themselves to this problem, and there is also evidence that consistent systems of proportion were used in the more distant past by Greek and Gothic designers. Research into the architecture of these periods shows constantly recurring mathematical relationships which could not have occurred by chance. If their use was the result of intuition, one would expect the same types of relationship to have appeared spontaneously in all periods of good design. In fact, this is not the case, and the sort of mathematical relationships which occur are closely related to the mathematical knowledge of the period.

If architects of the past, creating new styles of architecture based on new structural methods, used mathematical systems of proportion to help them, it is not surprising that an interest in the subject should again be common. The aim of the present study is to state a unified theory of proportion, and to show how it both arises out of, and helps to explain, the history of proportional theory in the past. The need for unification is obvious, as, in spite of the growing appreciation of the importance of the theory of proportion, and the growing volume of attention which is given to it, ideas on the subject remain confused.

There is, indeed, some excuse for the view that current theories contradict each other so violently as to cancel each other out, leaving nothing worthy of serious attention. Supporters of different proportional theories tell us on the one hand to use simple, easily intelligible ratios, and on the other hand to make our ratios subtle, not too obvious. Sometimes we are told to use geometry, and sometimes arithmetic. Although the golden section is nowadays the most popular key to good proportion, it is seldom that any attempt is made to compare its merits with those of its rivals.

The view which is put forward here is that these differences are superficial. Workers in this field of research have approached the subject from very different points of view, using different techniques, and the theories which they have elaborated appear to be so contradictory because they express only small parts of the truth. A theory which insists on the aesthetic superiority of the ratio of the golden section is difficult to reconcile with a theory which treats the simple ratios of musical consonance in the same manner. But the difficulty can be overcome if we regard these ratios not as aesthetic ends in themselves, but as alternative means to the same end.

These theories are like the pieces of a jigsaw puzzle which, taken a few at a time, form no coherent picture. But over the centuries quite a number of pieces have accumulated, and recently quite large patches of picture have begun to appear. What we hope to do here is not, perhaps, to complete the puzzle, but at least to establish the positions of the completed patches in the final picture, and to fit enough of the other loose pieces into place to suggest its general appearance.

Our subject is at one and the same time both narrowly technical and of the widest general interest. It overlaps with a variety of other subjects, such as metaphysics and metrology, music and morphology, anthropometry, archaeology and aesthetics. Although for many people these ramifications form the most fascinating aspect of the subject, we shall make most progress if we keep to the plain study of the theory of proportion.

It is, of course, neither possible nor desirable to avoid giving any attention to other considerations. We could not proceed very far without the use of mathematics, for instance, but we need not follow for their own sake lines of thought which are of purely mathematical interest. Again, in tracing the history of the subject, we shall inevitably have to take some notice of the endless discussions about the proportions of the human figure. We shall find, however, that we can usually treat experiments of this kind as exercises in various systems of proportion in art, ignoring their contradictory claims to reveal systems of proportion in nature.

A historical treatment of the subject is essential in order to show the present theory in its proper perspective. At first sight this may be rather surprising. It would not be necessary in presenting a physiological theory to go back to Vesalius or Aristotle, or in presenting a theory of mechanics to go back to Galileo or Archimedes. But in physiology and mechanics the progress of human thought has been fairly continuous, at least since the Renaissance. The discoveries of the past have been firmly incorporated in the knowledge of the present, and in stating a new theory, however revolutionary, we seldom have to retrace the steps by which our previous knowledge of the subject was gained.

In the theory of architecture the position is very different. It is not simply that progress has been slower than in some other fields of human thought, but it has been intermittent and at times almost completely interrupted. Thus if we were to confine ourselves to recent statements of architectural theory, we should be in danger of missing much of value which the Renaissance contributed, and which was thrown aside at the end of the eighteenth century.

The theory of proportion is part of the theory of architecture. The particular theory of proportion which is stated here is related to the history of the theory of proportion in general in two different ways. In the first place it is itself an outcome of the history. Its value depends largely on the degree to which it is based on the results of the long series of more or less successful experiments which form the history. It would therefore be reasonable to start with the history, and to show how the present theory can be regarded as developing out of it.

But the theory can also be considered as a possible key to the understanding of the history, and without some such key much of the history is unintelligible. For example, Giorgi's extraordinary application of Plato's 'Number of the World Soul' to architecture can be made sense of, not by sharing Giorgi's sympathy with Plato's metaphysics, but only through an understanding of the value of the geometric progression in architectural proportion.[1]

For this reason the present theory of proportion will be stated first in general outline. It will then become an easier matter to give a description of the history in the light of this theory, filling in the details of the theory as they are required. The success of the theory in explaining the historical development should give an indication of its value. We shall bring this historical account up to the present day, and try to complete it with a brief discussion of developments which are possible in the future. If, as Manning Robertson once remarked, the theory of proportion can be compared to a detective story,[2] what we are trying to do here is to give an explanation of the crime before we start to tell the story. This, though unusual, is not quite without precedent, and seems to be justified in the present case.

VISUAL PROPORTION

The first thing to be made clear is that we are concerned only with visual proportion, with the relationships of the shapes and sizes of objects which please the eye. Our theory must therefore be founded firmly on known facts about the kind of proportional relationships which are significant to the eye. It is important to distinguish quite clearly between visual proportion in this sense, which is purely a matter of pleasing the eye, and other considerations which affect the shapes and sizes of the parts of a design.

It has, indeed, often been denied that purely formal relationships of proportion give any satisfaction to the eye in themselves. For instance, the requirements of economical construction decide within certain limits the shapes and sizes of many parts of a building. It has been argued from time to time that the whole problem of proportion could be reduced to structural mechanics, and that engineering skill

[1] See p. 58 below. [2] 'The golden section or golden cut', *R.I.B.A. Journal* (October 1948).

could produce a unique, perfect and automatically pleasing solution to every problem of design. But the application of this theory in practice very quickly shows that the problem of making a building stand up is a different one from that of making it please the eye. The most that can be said is that any apparent defect in the construction of a building is likely to inhibit our enjoyment of its proportions.

A similar factor to structure, or 'firmness', in determining the proportions of a building, is 'commodity', or use. The purpose of a room, for instance, may determine its shape within certain limits. But it is very rarely the case that it determines it exactly, and normally it can be varied within fairly wide limits to take account of other requirements. In this case also our enjoyment of the proportions of the room is only inhibited if its shape is very obviously unsuitable for its purpose.

These two factors of structure and utility together constitute the 'fitness' which played an important part in debates on aesthetics and the theory of proportion in the eighteenth century. The attempt was often made by philosophers and critics to reduce the theory of proportion entirely to a theory of fitness. In fact, however, it is the common experience of designers in practice that when all the requirements of fitness have been met, a good deal of choice usually remains between proportions which appear pleasant and those which appear unpleasant.

Another factor which can be confused with visual proportion must be mentioned, especially as it seems to concern the eye very much more directly than fitness. This is the factor of custom or convention. It is obviously no use drawing a human figure in accordance with some canon of proportion if the result is not recognizable as a normal human being of the type which the eye is accustomed to see. In the same way when strong conventions are established in architecture, such as those controlling the proportions of the orders, any very marked departure from what the eye expects may destroy the pleasing effect of the design. The attempt has sometimes been made to reduce the theory of proportion entirely to a theory of custom or convention. This attempt was more likely to be successful in the Renaissance, when so much of architecture was controlled by custom, than it is today.

Indeed, the urgency of the need for an adequate theory of visual proportion today is partly due to the collapse of traditions in the face of new methods of construction and new uses for buildings. While it must be agreed that both fitness and custom may play an important part in determining proportions, it is very seldom in architecture that no latitude remains for the operation of visual proportion, that is, proportional relationships which please the eye in themselves, independently of external considerations such as fitness for purpose or agreement with convention.

One way of explaining the pleasing effect of proportion in architecture is to assume that certain shapes are more pleasing to the eye in themselves. Once the admired shapes have been selected—and this is where the difficulty lies—architectural proportion becomes a straightforward matter of using them as often as possible.

We shall find that in the Renaissance it was commonly believed that the most beautiful rectangles were those whose sides had the simple numerical relationships of musical consonance. More recently the most popular rectangle has been one whose sides are in the ratio of the golden section. Experiments to decide between the two have had rather inconclusive results, though they seem to have given a preference to the golden section. It is clear, however, that no individual rectangles are in themselves either outstandingly beautiful or outstandingly ugly. The secret of proportion seems to lie, not in the shapes themselves, but in the relationships between them. It would otherwise be difficult to explain how, for instance, the buildings of Palladio and those of Corbusier can both be well proportioned, when they embody quite different systems of shapes.[1]

The supposed beauty of certain individual shapes is not only a very doubtful assumption on which to base a theory of proportion, but it is also quite unnecessary. The use of these shapes in practice can be explained as a means to an end, and it is of no consequence whether the shapes themselves are regarded as beautiful or not. But before this is explained, we must first consider those proportional relationships which are, without any shadow of doubt, significant to the eye.

If we include sizes as well as shapes, there are three important relationships which the eye can, in fact, recognize. In the first place it possesses a remarkable power of recognizing the relationship between objects having the same shape. It can exercise this power whatever the distance of the objects, and to a large extent it can overcome the distortion caused by viewing the objects from different angles. The power of recognizing similar shapes is acquired very early in life, and is one on which we largely depend in finding our way about. The second relationship is that of objects having the same size as well as the same shape, but the recognition of this relationship demands comparatively favourable conditions. We can see at a glance that the sun and moon are of the same shape, but from the evidence of our eyes alone we might be tempted to think that they were of the same size as well; in looking at buildings, however, the eye can recognize this relationship fairly easily. Finally, there is the relationship of objects having the same size but different shapes. The recognition of this relationship seems to demand even more favourable conditions.

---

[1] The resemblance found by Colin Rowe in his 'Mathematics of the ideal villa' (*Architectural Review*, March 1947) between certain villas by Palladio and Corbusier appears to be accidental. The systems of proportion used by the two architects are, as we shall see, entirely different.

Of these three relationships the third is the least easily recognized and probably the least important; it will simplify the present discussion not to consider it in detail.[1] The second relationship, that of objects having the same size and shape, is fairly easily recognized. The repetition in design of elements of the same shape[2] and size leads to various types of symmetry: bilateral symmetry, radial symmetry, repeat symmetry and so on. The use of symmetry is well understood, and we need not consider it further here. We are left, then, with the first relationship, that of similarity of shape alone, as a possible key to the theory of proportion in architecture.

The importance of similarity of shape as a source of unity in design has seldom been denied. Its simplest and most familiar use in architecture lies in the repetition of some shape taken from the structural system. Obvious examples of this are the round arches and vaults of Roman and Romanesque architecture, and the pointed arches and vaults of Gothic architecture. We can thus give unity to a building by the repetition of one dominant shape in a number of its parts. Some writers have stressed the possibility of repeating the shape of a plan or elevation as a whole in the parts into which it is subdivided. In this case not only are certain of the parts related, but a still greater sense of order is achieved by relating these particular parts to the whole. Of course, it is not possible to make all the parts of a building similar in shape, even if such complete uniformity was desired, but the possibilities of introducing visible order are not exhausted by the repetition of one shape alone.

In a building where all the parts are of different shapes, the visual effect is one of the greatest possible disorder, indeed chaos. Order can be introduced by the repetition of similar shapes, and the highest degree of order results when comparatively few shapes are used, repeated as often as possible. This sort of order is clearly one which the eye can recognize. It is not a purely mathematical order which has to be consciously understood before it can be appreciated. We can therefore reasonably define the object of architectural proportion as the creation of visible order by the repetition of similar shapes.

This principle may at first sight appear too simple to account for all the facts; it seems, for instance, to throw no light on the use of particular shapes in architecture. But while the principle itself is extremely simple, its application in practice can become a very complicated matter. Once we decide to use a restricted number of shapes for all the parts of a design, the choice of these shapes is no longer an arbitrary affair. The smallest parts of the design add together to form

---

[1] But see p. 96 below for an example of this relationship.

[2] Strictly speaking we should distinguish shapes which are the same from those which are mirror images of each other, like those of a pair of hands.

larger parts, these larger parts form still larger ones, and eventually we come to the largest parts which add together to form the whole. If we select a limited group of shapes for the smaller parts quite arbitrarily, we have no reason to expect that the shapes of the larger parts will belong to the same limited group. We must therefore select a group of shapes which can be added together in the most varied ways without producing any new ones.

This additive property of shapes which we require is a little difficult to explain, but it is very easy to illustrate. Suppose that we start with a very simple group of shapes, the square and the double square. If two squares are added together, they form a double square. If two double squares are placed together side by side, they form a square. Two double squares can also be arranged with a square between them to form another double square. These additive properties of simple shapes like the square and double square explain why they could be used effectively in Renaissance architecture. And there are various other groups of shapes which behave in a similar way, like the group of shapes related to the golden section rectangle, or the group of shapes related to the $\sqrt{2}$ rectangle, whose longer side is equal to the diagonal of the square on the shorter side.

The choice of any particular shapes in architectural proportion need not, therefore, be explained by the supposed beauty of the shapes themselves. It may simply be due to the fact that certain groups of shapes can be used more readily than others to build up a pattern in which order and economy of form are apparent to the eye. The reasons why certain groups of shapes are more suitable for this purpose than others are mathematical. They can best be understood, not geometrically, but analytically, by reducing the problem from two or three dimensions to one. To do this we shall have to examine the relationships between visual proportion in the sense in which we have defined it, and mathematical proportion.

THE MATHEMATICS OF VISUAL PROPORTION

It will be convenient to restrict the discussion to problems of straight lines and rectangles. This will not be too unrealistic, as problems of this kind are those with which the modern architect is most often concerned.

Simple mathematical proportion consists of the equality of two ratios, e.g.

$$\frac{a}{b} = \frac{c}{d}.$$

The connexion between this type of proportion and similarity of shape is an obvious one over which we need not spend much time.

If we divide two straight lines of different lengths in the same ratio, we are making use of simple mathematical proportion. At the same time the equality of ratio is easily recognized by the eye. It can be said in a sense that the two figures which we have produced are of the same 'shape'. If we draw two rectangles of the same shape, the similarity of shape is again easily recognized. The ratios of the sides of the two rectangles are equal, so we have again made use of simple mathematical proportion. We may not have done so consciously, as we could use a geometrical method of drawing similar rectangles which does not require us to consider the relations between their linear dimensions. But whatever method we use, the linear dimensions will, in fact, conform to the pattern of simple mathematical proportion.

When we are dealing, not with separate rectangles, but with rectangles which are connected together in various ways, more complicated patterns of mathematical proportion may be developed among their linear dimensions. If, for instance, we draw two rectangles of the same shape but of different sizes, with one side in common, we are making use of continued proportion:

$$\frac{a}{b} = \frac{b}{c}.$$

If these ratios are equal to x, and if we make c equal to one unit of length, it is easy to see that the lengths of the sides of the rectangles become 1, x and x^2 units of length. The pattern of proportional relationships which has been generated between the linear dimensions is, in fact, that of a geometric progression.

It should be clear that the further we go in repeating similar shapes in a design, the more we tend to bind the linear dimensions of the design together in a pattern of relationships of mathematical proportion. In the simple case which we have just considered, it is the pattern of the single geometric progression which is generated:

$$1 \qquad a \qquad a^2 \qquad a^3 \quad \ldots$$

A slightly more complicated pattern is formed by two superimposed geometric progressions:

$$\begin{array}{cccc} 1 & a & a^2 & a^3 \quad \ldots \\ b & ab & a^2b & a^3b \quad \ldots \end{array}$$

A still more complicated pattern which includes the others as parts of itself is the double geometric progression:

$$\begin{array}{cccc} 1 & a & a^2 & a^3 \quad \ldots \\ b & ab & a^2b & a^3b \quad \ldots \\ b^2 & ab^2 & a^2b^2 & a^3b^2 \quad \ldots \\ b^3 & ab^3 & a^2b^3 & a^3b^3 \quad \ldots \\ \vdots & \vdots & \vdots & \vdots \end{array}$$

8

The solution of some problems of proportion may even require the use of a triple geometric progression.

If we use a scale of linear dimensions with a prearranged pattern of proportional relationships, like that of the geometric progression, it is a very simple matter to draw rectangles of the same shape but of different sizes, or of a limited number of shapes. The repetition of ratios embodied in the geometric progression leads to the repetition of shapes in two dimensions. What is perhaps not so obvious is that the converse is also true. The repetition of shapes in two dimensions leads to the repetition of ratios, and to the development of patterns of proportional relationships between the linear dimensions of the design.

The reader who is not satisfied with a general statement of this principle is invited to study the Appendix, where he will find concrete examples of the kind of things which happen when we start to introduce economy of form into a pattern of rectangles.

So far we have found nothing to decide what particular ratios are likely to be repeated, and what particular values can be given to a and b in our geometric progressions. Now it is not enough that the linear dimensions of a design should be connected by a pattern of proportional relationships. We have already seen how, in building up a design in two dimensions, the smaller parts must add up to form larger parts, and the larger parts must add up eventually to form a whole. For this to be possible, we must be able to add the linear dimensions together to form larger dimensions belonging to the same pattern of proportional relationships. Our geometric progressions, whether single or compound, must not only possess the normal property of embodying a pattern of repeated ratios. They must also possess a wide range of additive properties, by means of which smaller terms of the progressions can be added together to form larger terms.

As a matter of fact, only certain geometric progressions and combinations of geometric progressions have properties of this kind at all, and some have a richer variety of useful additive properties than others. It is therefore no accident that in tracing the history of our subject we shall find comparatively few patterns of proportional relationships, generated automatically or used deliberately in the solution of problems of architectural proportion.

Of these the simplest is the geometric progression:

$$1 \quad 2 \quad 4 \quad 8 \quad 16 \quad \ldots$$

This has only one set of additive properties: $1 + 1 = 2$, $2 + 2 = 4$, etc. One way of adding to them is to superimpose two geometric progressions:

$$1 \quad\quad 2 \quad\quad 4 \quad\quad 8 \quad\quad 16 \quad\quad \ldots$$
$$3 \quad\quad 6 \quad\quad 12 \quad\quad 24 \quad\quad \ldots$$

This has the additional sets of additive properties $1 + 2 = 3$, $2 + 4 = 6$, etc., and $1 + 3 = 4$, $2 + 6 = 8$, etc.

Another set of additive properties is given by adding a third geometric progression:

	1	2	4	8	16	...
		3	6	12	24	...
			9	18	...	

The additional additive properties are $1 + 8 = 9$, $2 + 16 = 18$, etc. We are well on the way here to a double geometric progression which we shall find playing an important part in the Renaissance theory of proportion, and which can be generated by the use of simple shapes like the square and double square. Its value is limited, however, by the rather restricted range of its additive properties.

Other progressions which occur in practice are based, not on whole numbers, but on square roots, such as the progression

$$1 \quad \sqrt{2} \quad 2 \quad 2\sqrt{2} \quad 4 \quad \ldots$$

This has the additive properties $1 + 1 = 2$, $\sqrt{2} + \sqrt{2} = 2\sqrt{2}$, etc. Then there is the related progression based on the number θ, which is equal to $1 + \sqrt{2}$, or $2 \cdot 414 \ldots$:

$$1 \quad \theta \quad \theta^2 \quad \theta^3 \quad \ldots$$

The characteristic additive property of this progression is $1 + 2\theta = \theta^2$.

These two progressions can be combined effectively in a double geometric progression based on θ and $\sqrt{2}$:

$$
\begin{array}{ccccc}
1 & \theta & \theta^2 & \theta^3 & \ldots \\
\sqrt{2} & \sqrt{2\theta} & \sqrt{2\theta^2} & \sqrt{2\theta^3} & \ldots \\
2 & 2\theta & 2\theta^2 & 2\theta^3 & \ldots \\
2\sqrt{2} & 2\sqrt{2\theta} & 2\sqrt{2\theta^2} & 2\sqrt{2\theta^3} & \ldots \\
\vdots & \vdots & \vdots & \vdots &
\end{array}
$$

This has a number of additive properties, including $1 + 1 = 2$, $1 + \sqrt{2} = \theta$, $1 + \theta = \sqrt{2\theta}$, $1 + 2\theta = \theta^2$, and $1 + \theta^2 = 2\sqrt{2\theta}$. The double geometric progression has thus not only the additive properties of the two single geometric progressions from which it is formed, but additional additive properties of its own as well; and we shall encounter several systems of proportion making use of the simple pattern of proportional relationships embodied in it. Their effectiveness is due to the fairly wide range of additive properties which it possesses.

Other systems of proportion produce different patterns of proportional relationships, such as the triple geometric progression based on the numbers $\sqrt{3}$, $1 + \sqrt{3}$

and 2, which may be generated, for instance, by the use of the 30°–60° and 45° set-squares.

Mention need only be made here of one more progression, which is probably the most valuable of them all. This is the geometric progression based on the number ϕ, which is equal to $\dfrac{1 + \sqrt{5}}{2}$, or 1·618.... It is the properties of this progression which account for the importance in architecture of the golden section, whose ratio is $\phi : 1$.

This geometric progression 1, ϕ, ϕ^2, ϕ^3, ..., has many useful additive properties of its own, of which $1 + \phi = \phi^2$ is the most important. But when it is combined with other progressions, its additive powers are so enormously increased that systems of proportion based upon it show a singular flexibility.

All the systems of proportion which we shall examine will be found to generate characteristic geometric progressions of the type which we have been discussing. Their value depends largely on the variety of additive properties which these geometric progressions possess. Judged from this point of view, systems based on whole numbers alone seem less likely to be effective than systems based on irrational numbers like ϕ and θ, and, of these, systems based on ϕ seem most likely to be effective.[1]

Finally, there is one more property of these numbers which must be described here. The numbers ϕ and θ are irrational, and their use in architecture produces dimensions which are incommensurable. This is clearly a disadvantage for ordinary architectural purposes, but it is one which can easily be overcome. The progression 1, ϕ, ϕ^2, ϕ^3, ... can be replaced by the Fibonacci series 1, 2, 3, 5, 8, 13, 21, ..., in which successive pairs of numbers are added together to form the next number. This series has exactly the same additive properties as the ϕ progression. It is not, of course, a true geometric progression, but the ratio of successive pairs of numbers approximates more and more closely to $\phi : 1$ as the series goes on. The Fibonacci series therefore forms a satisfactory whole-number substitute for the ϕ progression. The progression 1, θ, θ^2, θ^3, ... can be replaced in the same way by Pell's series, 1, 2, 5, 12, 29, ...

All of the progressions which have been mentioned here are of historical importance, although the part which they play in different systems of proportion has not always been clearly understood. Now that the relationship between mathematical proportion and visual proportion has been indicated, we are in a position to discuss the methods of applying mathematical proportion in practice.

---

[1] This argument is developed at greater length in the Appendix, where a fuller account of the properties of ϕ and θ is also given for readers who wish to pursue the subject in greater mathematical detail.

SYSTEMS OF PROPORTION IN PRACTICE

We have seen how economy of form in architecture can be achieved by the repetition of similar shapes. We have also seen that the repetition of similar shapes generates patterns of proportional relationships among the linear dimensions of the design. The study of these patterns helps to explain the use of individual shapes and groups of shapes. The use, for instance, of the ϕ rectangle, whose sides are in the ratio of the golden section, can be explained by the mathematical properties of the ϕ series. There is no need to introduce psychological, physiological or any other arguments to explain the importance of the golden section.

But the technique of analysing the relationships between linear dimensions is of value mainly in theory. A system of proportion in practice must not only lead to the flexible repetition of clearly defined shapes, but it must also be easy to use. Above all a designer must be able to use it without intricate mathematical calculations, just as the composer can use the scales of music without considering the mathematical relationships underlying them.

The systems of proportion which have been evolved can be classified in two different ways, either by the practical method which is used to put them into effect, or by the type of mathematical relationships which they embody. Classified according to practical method, these systems fall into two main groups. The first group consists of geometrical systems which aim directly at the repetition of similar shapes; patterns of proportional relationships develop automatically among the linear dimensions, but the designer is not immediately concerned with them. Systems of the second group aim indirectly at the repetition of similar shapes, through the use of linear dimensions with a prearranged pattern of proportional relationships. Systems of this type reduce the problem of proportion from the manipulation of shapes in two or three dimensions to the manipulation of lengths in one dimension at a time. They will therefore be described as analytical systems.

This difference in method can be seen, for instance, in the different ways of drawing a $\sqrt{2}$ rectangle, which plays an important part in many systems of proportion. Thus we can draw the rectangle in the traditional way by making the longer side equal to the diagonal of the square on the shorter side, or we can construct it much more quickly by using one of R's set-squares. These are both geometrical methods. But we can equally well calculate the lengths of the sides of the rectangle arithmetically and use an ordinary scale in drawing them, or we can save time by using a specially prepared scale of dimensions based on the geometric progression $1, \sqrt{2}, 2, \ldots$. These are both analytical methods.

Geometrical systems of proportion give the designer direct control over the shapes which he is using, but the linear dimensions of the design are left to take care of themselves. The architect, however, is very much concerned with these dimensions, some of which are given in his programme, and all of which must be determined before his design can be carried out. He may therefore very well prefer to use an analytical system for most purposes.

The other way of classifying systems of proportion is to divide them into systems using dimensions which are commensurable, and which are related by geometric progressions based on whole numbers, and systems using dimensions which are often incommensurable, and which are related by geometric progressions based on other numbers like ϕ or θ. We can conveniently call these systems 'commensurable' and 'incommensurable' systems, and the ratios which occur in them 'commensurable' and 'incommensurable' ratios.[1] With few exceptions incommensurable systems can be divided again into systems based on the numbers $\sqrt{2}$ and $1 + \sqrt{2}$, or θ, systems based on the numbers $\sqrt{3}$ and $1 + \sqrt{3}$, which is not common enough to require a special name, and finally systems based on the numbers $\sqrt{5}$ and $\dfrac{1 + \sqrt{5}}{2}$, or ϕ.

We have already seen that commensurable systems are likely to be less flexible in practice than incommensurable systems, because of the small number of useful additive properties possessed by geometric progressions based on whole numbers alone. For this reason geometrical systems are usually incommensurable, like R's set-squares or the geometry of root-rectangles which Hambidge attributes to the Greeks of the classical period. The geometrical system using commensurable ratios is rare, though Hambidge finds traces of it in early Greek work.

On the other hand, analytical systems have tended in the past to be commensurable, because of the difficulty of manipulating incommensurable ratios except by geometrical methods; the analytical and commensurable type of system was common in the Renaissance. However, the difficulty of using an analytical system which is also incommensurable has been overcome, and Corbusier's Modulor provides an example of this type of system.

This method of classifying the different systems of proportion used in practice is essential for the study of the history of proportion with which we shall now be concerned. We shall see how first one type of system became important and then another. We shall also see that whatever strange theoretical ideas on the subject of proportion may have been entertained at various periods, the practical systems which were actually used can be explained, and their merits compared, by means of the theory which has been stated here in outline.

[1] This distinction between 'commensurable' and 'incommensurable' systems of proportion corresponds in some ways to Hambidge's distinction between static symmetry and dynamic symmetry (see pp. 116–7 below).

In studying the history of the theory of proportion a question of the greatest importance arises at the start, and that is the question of what kind of evidence is to be considered acceptable.

History, strictly speaking, is the study of periods for which written records are available, and the rest is archaeology. The history of the theory of proportion is complicated for us by the fact that even highly literate peoples like the Greeks have left no surviving records describing the systems of proportion which they used.

In general, three types of evidence are available. The first consists of direct literary evidence, supplemented occasionally by actual drawings showing how architects applied systems of proportion in practice. The only surviving literary evidence from antiquity is the work of Vitruvius. Since the Renaissance there has been a fairly continuous literature devoted to the theory of proportion in architecture.

The second type of evidence consists of indirect literary evidence. The literature of mathematics and, to a much lesser extent, that of philosophy provide valuable clues as to the ideas on proportion current in periods from which no direct literary evidence survives.

Finally, there is archaeological evidence, consisting of the remains of buildings or other surviving works of art. At first sight the analysis of the actual proportions of architecture would seem to be the most direct way to a knowledge of the system of proportion employed by the designer. Experience has shown, however, that the difficulties of correct analysis are enormous; there are, for instance, innumerable analyses of the proportions of the Parthenon, each claiming to prove that a different system of proportion was used by the Greeks. Evidence of this type is therefore extremely unreliable, and is only worth considering when it is strongly supported by evidence of some other type. Thus Hambidge's analysis of the Parthenon seems to be of value, not only on internal grounds, but because the system of proportion which Hambidge reconstructs is closely related to the sort of mathematical problems in which we know the Greeks were interested.

The problem of what kind of evidence is to be accepted is related to that of the order of presentation of history: if we adopt a strictly chronological order of presentation, the work of Vitruvius, which should form an introduction to the Renaissance, would be separated from it by a highly speculative account of a very different system of proportion which is believed to have been used in the Middle Ages. We cannot entirely ignore the periods for which little or no direct literary evidence is available, as this would give a wholly distorted picture of the history of the theory of proportion. There is, however, no need to give them a full and separate treatment. We shall therefore confine ourselves for the most part to the firm ground of theories and systems of proportion for which there is direct literary evidence.

We shall start with the difficult task of giving an interpretation of Vitruvius, and then proceed direct to the Renaissance. Throughout these two periods we shall mainly be concerned with analytical systems of proportion based on the use of commensurable ratios. From the beginning of the nineteenth century onwards we shall find geometrical systems based on the use of incommensurable ratios becoming more important. We shall also find that the advocates of these systems believed that they had rediscovered systems used by Greek or Gothic architects. We shall therefore be able to avoid the distortion which would be caused by omitting the Greek and Gothic periods altogether, but we shall be dealing with them mainly at second hand. Finally, in the twentieth century, we shall find systems of a new type, analytical and yet based on the use of incommensurable ratios, which can claim to combine the advantages of the main systems of the past.

CHAPTER II

VITRUVIUS AND THE THEORY
OF PROPORTION

Professor Wittkower tells us that 'Vitruvius' work contains no real theory of proportion'.[1] It is true that Vitruvius, in spite of his interest in the subject, fails to pass on to us a coherent theory, either of his own or borrowed from the Greek authorities to whom he often refers. While he gives us an encyclopaedic account of Roman building and engineering practice, his observations on the theory of architecture and particularly on the theory of proportion appear to us at times almost nonsensical.

Newton, in his footnote to the description of architecture,[2] says that 'all the commentators of Vitruvius allow this explication of architecture to be very dark and unintelligible, and all differ in their interpretation thereof....The words are here put together in such a manner as seems to us to have no coherence or sense....' Now this may be because Vitruvius was a practical man, not a theorist, and the theoretical part of his work may be merely a garbled account of Greek theories which he failed to understand, but with which he hoped to impress his readers. Newton, however, blames not Vitruvius, but the fact that the meanings of the words have been lost.

While Vitruvius' work may be a broken link in the chain of communication between us and the Greeks, it is not the only link in the chain. It is worth while inquiring whether the fault may not rest with one of the others.

If the text was seriously mutilated between the date when it was written and the date of the earliest manuscript, the Harleian 2767, there is nothing that can be done about it. But Professor Granger believes that this manuscript was written early enough to have escaped the purist revisions of the Carolingian period.[3]

There were no commentaries in the medieval period, and the study of Vitruvius seems to have had a completely fresh start in the Renaissance. It is not therefore surprising that the meanings of words had been lost, that commentators had to struggle to interpret apparently unintelligible passages, or that their perplexity is shared by us today.

---

[1] *Architectural Principles in the Age of Humanism*, 2nd ed. p. 120.
[2] *De architectura* (transl. Newton, 1791), I, ii, 1. [3] *De architectura* (1931), vol. I, p. xviii.

Our understanding of Vitruvius is largely based on the Renaissance interpretation of his work. Now this interpretation contains at least one possible source of error, which would particularly affect an understanding of Vitruvius' theory of proportion. The humanists of the early Renaissance were neo-Platonists, regarding the work of Plato as the flower of classical culture. Few of them, it is true, made very much sense of Vitruvius' ideas on proportion. But Cardan, in the sixteenth century, attributed to him a theory of proportion based on an analogy with music.[1] The 'musical analogy' or 'harmonic' theory of proportion was, as Professor Wittkower shows,[2] derived in the Renaissance from Plato's *Timaeus*. Now although there is no trace in Vitruvius of any analogy between musical harmony and architectural proportion, Cardan's error reappears from time to time in various forms.

It is obvious that Vitruvius himself was no neo-Platonist. He pays his proper respects to Plato by including him in his lists of noted philosophers,[3] and gives the treatment of the duplication of the square from the *Meno*,[4] but this he praises for its *utility*,[5] a compliment which Plato himself might not have appreciated. On the other hand, he refers as often and with equal respect to the ideas of the opposing school of Democritus. It may therefore be worth while to start to search afresh for a 'real theory of proportion' in Vitruvius.

PROPORTION IN GENERAL

In looking for a real theory of proportion, we are of course mainly interested in the aesthetic aspect of proportion. Much of what Vitruvius wrote on proportion is, however, concerned with the relationships of the shapes and sizes of objects considered from quite a different point of view, as a reading of his work will show. When, for instance, he speaks of the 'symmetries' and 'proportions' of catapults,[6] he is not displaying a quaint interest in the aesthetics of slaughter. He is merely telling us how to make a catapult of a shape which has been found to work, and of a size proportioned to the length of the arrow we wish to shoot from it.

The use of the module itself has no necessary aesthetic significance. It may be simply a useful practical device for describing the comparative sizes of an object and its parts, without fixing the absolute measurements. By giving us the proportions of an order in terms of a module, Vitruvius enables us to construct it to any size we wish. Usually it is only when speaking of an actual example, such as his own

---

[1] See p. 36 below.
[2] *Architectural Principles in the Age of Humanism*, 2nd ed. pp. 90 ff.
[3] *De architectura* (1931), VII, pref. 2; IX, pref. 2.   [4] *Ibid.* IX, pref. 4, 5.
[5] *Ibid.* IX, pref. 4, '...e multis ratiocinationibus utilissimis'; IX, pref. 15, '...ad omnium utilitatem'.
[6] *Ibid.* X, X, 1.

basilica at Fano,[1] that he gives the measurements in feet. If he had not written down lists of comparative measurements in this way, half the value of his work would have been lost with the illustrations.

Proportional relationships cover the whole field of architecture, and they can be considered from the point of view of commodity and firmness as well as that of delight. This Vitruvius does. In describing the proportions of the elevations of temples he finds that the pycnostyle and the systyle lack commodity, and the diastyle firmness.[2] The proportions of a Doric column resemble those of a man's body in strength as well as grace.[3]

In his description of the plans of houses, Vitruvius takes the unusual step of varying the proportions according to the actual size of the atrium, 'with a view both to use and to effect'.[4] There seems, however, to be no example of this being done with a view to firmness. The principle of a quantitative increase in size requiring for structural reasons a qualitative change in proportions, which helps to explain the difference in shape between a gazelle and an elephant, may not have been known to Vitruvius. On the other hand, the orders were sturdy enough to be used up to a great size, and in their case the economy of adjusting shape to size may have been consciously rejected on aesthetic grounds.[5]

It is clear, then, that many of Vitruvius' frequent references to proportion had nothing to do with its aesthetic aspect, which can itself be approached from two quite different points of view. The first of these is the intuitive approach, in which the proportions of an object are modified to please the eye through a slow process of trial and error. In architecture this process may extend over many generations in the gradual refinement of traditional forms. In painting and sculpture the process may take the form of the selection of the most admired proportions from nature. In either case two forces are at work, the desire of the eye for what Wren calls 'customary beauty', the traditional or life-like, and its simultaneous desire for 'natural beauty', the harmony of proportion 'achieved in such a manner that nothing could be added or taken away or altered except for the worse'.[6] The other approach lies in the conscious application of a theory of proportion.

There is no evidence that Vitruvius distinguished clearly between the two approaches. In his practical examples of the orders he seems to be giving us traditional proportions evolved by the Greeks, but in his theoretical statements he appears to have some theory of proportion in his mind. It would be unwise to hope

[1] *De architectura* (1931), V, i, 6 ff.　　　[2] *Ibid.* III, iii, 3–4.

[3] *Ibid.* IV, i, 6.　　　[4] *Ibid.* VI, iii, 5.

[5] See chapter on proportion in Percy E. Nobbs's *Design: a Treatise on the Discovery of Form* (1937).

[6] Alberti, quoted in Wittkower, 2nd ed., *Architectural Principles in the Age of Humanism* (1952), p. 29.

to recover a theory wholly from the practical examples. Any theory which Vitruvius held must be sought in the 'dark and unintelligible' passages in the description of architecture,[1] and in the long and equally mystifying discussion of proportion which introduces the reader to temple-planning.[2]

WORDS WITH LOST MEANINGS

Before the possible meanings of these passages are discussed, something must be said about the meanings of individual words which seem to have been lost. The words whose meanings have been most completely confused are 'symmetria', 'eurythmia', 'proportio' and 'commensus', all of which have been translated into English by one translator or another as 'proportion'.

'Proportio' is almost invariably translated as 'proportion'. 'Symmetria' is translated consistently as 'symmetry' by Newton[3] and Morgan,[4] as 'symmetry', 'proportion' or 'harmony' by Granger,[5] and as 'symmetry', 'proportion' or 'uniformity' by Gwilt.[6] The common phrase 'proportiones et symmetriae' is usually translated as 'proportions and symmetries'.

The words 'eurythmia' and 'commensus' are less common. 'Eurythmia' is translated by Newton as 'eurythmy', by Gwilt as 'proportion', by Granger as 'proportion' or 'eurythmy', and by Morgan as 'harmony' or 'eurythmy'. 'Commensus' has been variously translated as 'proportion', 'measure', 'measurement', 'dimension', 'adjustment', 'correspondence' and 'scale'.

The confusion apparent here is increased by the fact that 'proportion', 'symmetry' and 'harmony' have a variety of overlapping meanings in English, while 'eurythmy' has no recognized meaning at all. These facts enable the translators to produce renderings which are not obviously nonsense, although unfortunately they convey very little sense. In some ways the most satisfactory solution to the problem of translation seems to be that of Newton, who consistently uses anglicized forms of the Latin words, however odd they sound, and adds explanatory footnotes to help the reader in the difficult task of sorting out the meaning.

Now it is quite probable that Vitruvius did in fact mean different, clearly distinguished, things by the words he used. We cannot expect him to be entirely consistent in the use of words, especially as he was trying to translate Greek ideas into Latin words. But in these circumstances he was more likely to be forced to give several meanings to one word, than to attach several words to one meaning.

The word 'proportio', for instance, is given by Vitruvius as the Latin equivalent of the Greek word ἀναλογία. Professor Ghyka[7] regards this as the equality of two

---

[1] *De architectura* (1931), I, ii.   [2] *Ibid.* III, i.   [3] *Ibid.* (1791).
[4] *Ibid.* (1914).   [5] *Ibid.* (1931).   [6] *Ibid.* (1826).
[7] Article, 'Le Corbusier's Modulor', in *Architectural Review* (February 1948).

ratios, and Euclid himself used the word consistently in this sense. But in the lighter literature of Greek mathematics, exemplified by Nicomachus,[1] who was more nearly a contemporary of Vitruvius, ἀναλογία is used in several senses, including that of ratio itself as well as the equality of ratios. It is possible that this multiplicity of meaning is retained in Vitruvius' use of the word 'proportio', just as it is in the English word 'proportion'.[2] The word συμμετρία is also used in many different senses by Greek writers, including 'commensurability', 'symmetry', 'proportion', 'suitable relation' and 'convenient size'.

The only way of selecting the meanings of the words used by Vitruvius is to study their contexts. In the first place a clue is provided by the frequently recurring phrase 'proportiones et symmetriae'. There can be little doubt that this means 'proportions' in the sense of comparative sizes. The individual words 'proportiones' and 'symmetriae' may be used here merely as synonyms, but, on the other hand, they may mean 'comparative sizes' defined in different ways.

Now there are in fact two quite different ways of measuring comparative sizes which Vitruvius himself uses. In his definition of 'symmetria' he makes it fairly clear that the 'symmetries' are worked out in terms of a part, or module.[3] In his discussion of 'proportio' he gives as an illustration the comparative sizes of the parts of a human figure worked out in terms of the whole.[4] It therefore seems reasonable to distinguish between 'proportiones', the sizes of parts compared to the size of the whole, and 'symmetriae', the sizes of parts compared to a smaller part or module. The words 'proportio' and 'symmetria' are also used in more general senses, related in rather a complicated way. We shall have to try to explain, for instance, why proportion must be adjusted to symmetry,[5] and why symmetry depends on proportion, which is required for working out the 'symmetries'.[6]

In discussing Vitruvius' theory it will be convenient to start with 'proportio'. We can then go on to inquire how 'symmetria' depends on it. For the purpose of understanding his theory the meanings of 'commensus' and 'eurythmia' are less important. 'Commensus' perhaps means comparative size in general, and Vitruvius himself defines 'eurythmia' as the graceful appearance produced by the use of suitable proportions[7]. It is perhaps not too far-fetched to suggest that to the Greeks it may have suggested even more, gracefulness caused by the 'rhythmic recurrence of the same ratios'.[8]

---

[1] Nicomachus' *Introduction to Arithmetic*, translated by M. L. d'Ooge (New York, 1926).

[2] The difficulty was later overcome by Boethius, who used 'proportio' for ratio and 'proportionalitas' for proportion. Cf. Italian Renaissance 'proportione' and 'proportionalità', German 'Proporzion' and 'Proporzionalität'.   [3] *De architectura* (1931), I, ii, 4, '...e membris invenitur symmetriarum ratiocinatio'.

[4] *Ibid*. III, i, 1, 2.   [5] *Ibid*. I, ii, 2.   [6] *Ibid*. III, i, 1.

[7] *Ibid*. I, ii, 3.   [8] Walter Dorwin Teague, *Design This Day* (1946), p. 126.

THE THEORY OF PROPORTION

Vitruvius' theory of proportion is discussed most fully in the opening chapter of book III. Confusing as the chapter is, it is clear that the subject under discussion is the aesthetic aspect of proportion, and not one of the other aspects which have been mentioned. The chapter contains the famous section on the proportions of the human figure, which had such a powerful influence in the Renaissance. Vitruvius says that the proportions of a temple ought to be like those of a well-formed human figure, which he proceeds to describe in some detail.

Now it has often been assumed that the stress here should be on the human figure itself, and on its natural proportions. Advocates of different systems of proportion have argued that Vitruvius was quite right about this, but that nature happens to have designed the human figure according to their own favoured system.[1]

Vitruvius himself is no doubt responsible for the irrelevance of the argument over the natural proportions of the human figure, since he first brought nature into the discussion. But his remarks make much more sense if we treat his human figure as a vivid diagram, so familiar that it does not need to be drawn, which he uses to illustrate the sort of proportions which he advocated for design in general. The stress then falls, not on the human figure itself, but on the actual proportions given to it.

These proportions agree with our interpretation, as they express the size of the parts in terms of the whole. What is remarkable about them is the fact that all the sizes of the parts are *submultiples* of the size of the whole, and that the proportions are not merely commensurable, but consist of unit fractions.[2] It is in this simple mathematical fact that the key to Vitruvius' system of proportion lies, not in any neo-Platonic conceptions.

If the size of the whole, in this case the height of the human figure, is M units, and the sizes of the parts are submultiples of this, all the sizes belong to a *harmonic* scale descending from the size of the whole:

$$M \quad M/2 \quad M/3 \quad M/4 \quad M/5 \quad M/6 \quad M/7 \quad M/8 \quad M/9 \quad M/10 \quad \dots$$

This is a scale of 'preferred dimensions'. It does not in itself constitute a real system of proportion, since the use of this scale, based on the harmonic progression, favours the repetition of ratios no more than the use of an ordinary scale based on an arithmetic progression.

The attempt to attribute to Vitruvius a system of proportion more effective than this will rest on rather more slender evidence. It should not, however, surprise us

[1] Cf. Hambidge in *Dynamic Symmetry: the Greek Vase* (1920).
[2] Note the importance of the unit fraction in Egyptian arithmetic.

that it is difficult to recover what Vitruvius had in mind. Our knowledge of the practical mathematical technique of the Greeks, as opposed to their mathematical theory, is comparatively limited. Encyclopaedic as he set out to make his account of architecture, Vitruvius was not writing a mathematical text-book. He could reasonably omit a detailed account of the mathematical technique of proportion, contenting himself with a statement of general principles. These seem nonsense only to people lacking the knowledge of technique which his contemporary readers possessed.

One clue which can be followed up is the fact that in his example Vitruvius does not extend his harmonic progression indefinitely, but only as far as $M/10$. The sizes of the smaller subdivisions of the human figure are calculated, not as submultiples of the size of the whole itself, but as submultiples of the size of the part of which they are smaller parts. Here again Vitruvius does not say this explicitly, but he does it himself by subdividing the face into three parts.[1] It is true of course that the sizes of these smaller parts are still submultiples of the size of the whole as well, in this case $M/30$. But what Vitruvius is doing, consciously or not, is to ensure a proportional relationship between the sizes of the smaller parts and those of the larger.

A simpler example will make this clear. Let us suppose that the initial harmonic progression, instead of being carried as far as $M/10$, is stopped at $M/4$, and that secondary harmonic progressions are formed by subdividing each of these dimensions in exactly the same way.

The initial progression is:

$$M/1 \quad M/2 \quad M/3 \quad M/4.$$

The secondary progressions, written downwards, are:

$$M/2 \quad M/4 \quad M/6 \quad M/8$$
$$M/3 \quad M/6 \quad M/9 \quad M/12$$
$$M/4 \quad M/8 \quad M/12 \quad M/16$$

Some of the dimensions are repeated. If these are eliminated, the table can be rewritten as follows:

$$M/1 \quad M/2 \quad M/4 \quad M/8 \quad M/16$$
$$M/3 \quad M/6 \quad M/12$$
$$M/9$$

Here at last is an instrument of proportion, a scale of dimensions based on a double geometric progression with additive properties, derived from the original harmonic progression. Its use will lead automatically to the repetition of a limited number of ratios and therefore of shapes.

[1] *De architectura* (1931), III, i, 2.

If the initial harmonic progression is taken as far as $M/6$, the table of secondary harmonic progressions becomes

$M/1$	$M/2$	$M/3$	$M/4$	$M/5$	$M/6$
$M/2$	$M/4$	$M/6$	$M/8$	$M/10$	$M/12$
$M/3$	$M/6$	$M/9$	$M/12$	$M/15$	$M/18$
$M/4$	$M/8$	$M/12$	$M/16$	$M/20$	$M/24$
$M/5$	$M/10$	$M/15$	$M/20$	$M/25$	$M/30$
$M/6$	$M/12$	$M/18$	$M/24$	$M/30$	$M/36$

which can be written in the form of a triple geometric progression:

$M/1$	$M/2$	$M/4$	$M/8$	$M/16$
$M/3$	$M/6$	$M/12$	$M/24$	
$M/5$	$M/10$	$M/20$		
$M/9$	$M/18$	$M/36$		
$M/15$	$M/30$			
$M/25$				

We can carry these initial and secondary harmonic progressions as far as we like. But each time a fresh prime number is added to them, an extra dimension is added to the resulting geometric progression, which gradually loses its value in providing a simple pattern of proportional relationships.

The reader may complain that if this is what Vitruvius meant, there was nothing to stop him saying so in general terms, instead of giving us a vague practical example and leaving us to draw our own conclusions. But it must be remembered that this had been common practice in the work of Egyptian mathematicians for thousands of years. The great theoretical stride from the use of concrete mathematical examples to the mathematical statement in general terms had been taken very few centuries before Vitruvius' time by the Greeks, and was still found only in the writings of rigorous mathematicians.

Finally, a practical example of this method of proportion applied to architecture is afforded by the Attic base which Vitruvius describes.[1] The dimensions are expressed in terms of the diameter of the column:

Thickness of base with plinth	$\frac{1}{2}$
Diameter of column	1
Projection or 'ecphora'	$\frac{1}{6}$
Width of base	$1\frac{1}{2}$
Height of base without plinth	$\frac{1}{3}$

[1] *De architectura* (1931), III, V, 1, 2.

Height of plinth	$\frac{1}{2} - \frac{1}{3} = \frac{1}{6}$
Height of upper torus	$\frac{1}{4} \times \frac{1}{3} = \frac{1}{12}$
Height of base without plinth or upper torus	$\frac{3}{4} \times \frac{1}{3} = \frac{1}{4}$
Height of lower torus	$\frac{1}{2} \times \frac{1}{4} = \frac{1}{8}$

In this example no harmonic progression is carried beyond the submultiple of $\frac{1}{6}$, and the submultiple of $\frac{1}{5}$ is excluded, so the pattern of proportional relationships is unusually simple for Vitruvius. It consists of a double geometrical progression:

$$
\begin{array}{ccccc}
 & 1\frac{1}{2} & & & \\
1 & \frac{1}{2} & \frac{1}{4} & \frac{1}{8} & \\
\frac{1}{3} & \frac{1}{6} & \frac{1}{12} & &
\end{array}
$$

But for a fuller understanding of Vitruvius' theory we must now turn to a discussion of the obscure relationship between proportion and symmetry.

PROPORTION AND SYMMETRY

So far the discussion has been confined to 'proportion', or the relationship of the sizes of the parts to the sizes of the whole. But Vitruvius makes it quite clear that 'symmetry' is required as well: 'Namque non potest aedis ulla sine symmetria atque proportione rationem habere compositionis....'[1]

We have already seen that in his definition of symmetry he explains that it depends on the use of a module.[2] Just as 'proportion' seems to suggest the use of a scale based on the harmonic progression, so 'symmetry' in this sense may imply the use of a scale based on the use of the arithmetic progression:

$$m \quad 2m \quad 3m \quad 4m \quad 5m \quad 6m \quad 7m \quad 8m \quad 9m \quad 10m \quad \dots$$

It would be possible to extract a system of proportion from the arithmetic progression just as we have extracted one from the harmonic progression. But we are not faced here with the problem of choosing between harmonic and arithmetic scales, which became important in the Renaissance. For Vitruvius explains that 'symmetry' is not merely a matter of using modules, but that it depends on 'proportion' as well: 'Aedium compositio constat ex symmetria, cuius rationem diligentissime architecti tenere debent. Ea autem paritur a proportione, quae graece *analogia* dicitur.'[3] Elsewhere he speaks of the adjustment of 'proportion' to 'symmetry', 'proportionis ad symmetriam comparatio'.[4]

The exact meaning of these passages is obscure, and the translations do not help us very much. But the following explanation seems to make sense of the broad lines

---

[1] *De architectura* (1931), III, i, 1.   [2] *Ibid.* I, ii, 4.
[3] *Ibid.* III, i, 1.   [4] *Ibid.* I, ii, 2.

of the argument. 'Symmetry' in a building depends on the use of dimensions which can be expressed in terms of the size of a particular part, or module. But it also depends on the principle of 'proportion', by means of which the sizes of all the parts are related to the size of the whole. It should not merely be possible to express the 'symmetries', or comparative sizes of the parts of a building in terms of a module, but these sizes must also be aliquot parts of the size of the whole.

The result of fulfilling both these conditions is highly interesting, and can best be shown by a practical example. Let us, like Vitruvius, take a man for our example. Instead of 96 Roman digits, his height can well be 72 English inches. The use of this module alone would simply give us a scale of inches for the dimensions of the man based on all the numbers from 1 to 72. The principle of 'proportion' requires us to reject those numbers which are not submultiples of 72. The following numbers remain:

$$1 \quad 2 \quad 3 \quad 4 \quad 6 \quad 8 \quad 9 \quad 12 \quad 18 \quad 24 \quad 36 \quad 72$$

These are, of course, the factors of 72, including 1 and 72 itself. It is obvious that there exists between them a simple pattern of proportional relationships, which can be displayed by arranging them in the form of the familiar double geometric progression:

$$
\begin{array}{cccc}
1 & 2 & 4 & 8 \\
3 & 6 & 12 & 24 \\
9 & 18 & 36 & 72 \\
\end{array}
$$

If the multiples of the module are replaced by submultiples of the whole, it becomes clear that the method gives very similar results to those obtained by the method of secondary harmonic progressions:

$$
\begin{array}{cccc}
1/72 & 1/36 & 1/18 & 1/9 \\
1/24 & 1/12 & 1/6 & 1/3 \\
1/8 & 1/4 & 1/2 & 1 \\
\end{array}
$$

If, instead of dividing the height of the man into 72 modules, we divide it into 120 modules, the progression is given by the factors of 120. It can be expressed in the same way in the form either of 'symmetries' or of 'proportions':

'SYMMETRIES'				'PROPORTIONS'			
1	2	4	8	1/120	1/60	1/30	1/15
3	6	12	24	1/40	1/20	1/10	1/5
5	10	20	40	1/24	1/12	1/6	1/3
15	30	60	120	1/8	1/4	1/2	1

In this case the pattern is slightly more complicated, and consists of part of a triple geometric progression. The scale of 'proportions' includes all those which Vitruvius gives in his own specification for a human figure:

$$1 \quad 1/4 \quad 1/6 \quad 1/8 \quad 1/10 \quad 1/3 \times 1/10 = 1/30$$

It could therefore be used for determining the proportions of the parts of the body which he leaves unspecified.[1]

The study of Vitruvius has led us here to a flexible system of proportion which may perhaps be of more than historical interest, and which enables us to tailor a scale of preferred dimensions to the job in hand. Given the largest dimension of an object, we must choose a convenient module, deciding the number of modules contained in the given dimension. The factors of this number will, if the module is suitably chosen,[2] form a multiple geometric progression which gives us a scale of dimensions. The scale includes, of course, the dimension with which we started, and it can be extended in any direction.

It may be argued that in practice Vitruvius' examples seldom have the simplicity of this system. But these examples are, as we have seen, based on the traditionally evolved forms of the orders, to which a mathematical scheme of proportion would not necessarily apply. The fact that he meant something more than a vague generalization by his account of symmetry and proportion is shown by his references to weights and measures and perfect numbers. We shall now see how far our explanation of his theory helps to explain them.

WEIGHTS AND MEASURES

The interpretation of Vitruvius' system of proportion which has just been given is admittedly based on slender direct evidence. It does, however, transform the rest of Vitruvius' chapter on proportion, including the discussion of weights and measures, from an irrelevant and meaningless interpolation into a valuable historical theory of proportion.

Vitruvius has started the third chapter of his third book by stressing the im-

---

[1] 'Reliqua quoque membra suas habent commensus proportiones...' (III, i, 2). It is to supply some of the remaining proportions that Barbaro quotes from book XI of Cardan's *De subtilitate* in a footnote to his own version of Vitruvius (1567, p. 89). Cardan himself divides the height of the man into 180 modules, and states the comparative sizes of the parts as 'symmetries', or multiples of the module. Barbaro gives them as 'proportions', or submultiples of the whole height, as well: 1 (1/180), 2 (1/90), 4 (1/45), 6 (1/30), 12 (1/15), 24 (1/7½), 18 (1/10), 36 (1/5), 30 (1/6), 180 (1). He seems to have been feeling his way towards the system of proportion described above.

[2] Much depends on the choice of a module which will give a number with sufficient factors to form a useful scale, such as 36, 60, 120 or 144. The problem is related to that of choosing a base for a system of numeration.

portance of proportion, especially in the design of temples, 'in which the excellencies and faults remain for ever'.[1] He has given us a hint as to the system of proportion to use in his vivid illustration taken from the human figure, and prepared us for what is coming next.

It is obvious that the system which he has in mind is an *analytical* system, based not on the geometry of the Greeks, but on the manipulation of linear dimensions. It is also obvious that the linear dimensions involved are *commensurable*.[2] The details of the system would of course be familiar to his readers, and it is naturally difficult for us to reconstruct them. But it is highly probable that the system is a 'real' one, involving the use of dimensions having a definite pattern of proportional relationships, that of the multiple geometric progression,[3] and therefore favouring the repetition of certain ratios and shapes, and the introduction of visible order into design.

If this is true, it is easy to explain what Vitruvius is doing in the remainder of the chapter. He is giving an extremely interesting historical explanation of how just such a system of proportion could have evolved in practice, without at first any conscious intention in the minds of its users.

Architecture, much more than painting, pottery or sculpture, is a co-operative art, the work of many men. In order that men can co-operate in this art, in order, for instance, that the joiner can make a window frame to fill the opening left by the mason, and that both can work to the design of the architect, they need a language of size, a system of measures. Logically, only one measure is required, such as the foot or metre, used in conjunction with an effective system of numeration. This, however, presupposes the existence on the one hand of simple methods of arithmetical calculation, and on the other hand of a reasonably high general level of mathematical education. To the Egyptian, burdened by clumsy methods of arithmetic and a low standard of mathematical literacy outside the priestly class, such a method would be impracticable.

The earliest tendency would be to develop a system of many measures, each one with a name of its own. And, as Vitruvius points out, such a system was ready to hand in the measures of the human body: 'Nec minus mensurarum rationes, quae in

---

[1] *De architectura* (1791), III, i, 4.

[2] Note, however, certain 'islands' of geometry and incommensurability which occur in Vitruvius' work. Hambidge suggests that these are probably survivals from the Greek classical period, and believes that their importance was first noticed by Hay. They include the use of the $\sqrt{2}$ rectangle in the Corinthian capital (IV, i, 11) and in the courtyards of houses (VI, iii, 3).

[3] The Greek and Roman world was quite familiar with the double geometric progression. Nicomachus gives examples of it in order to help his readers in the study of Plato's *Timaeus* (*Introduction to Arithmetic*, II, iii and iv).

omnibus operibus videntur necessariae esse, ex corporis membris collegerunt, uti digitum, palmum, pedem, cubitum. ...'[1] To digit, palm, foot and cubit we can add inch, pace, yard, ell, hand, span, fathom, and others which are derived directly, or like the inch indirectly, from the human body. In periods of low mathematical literacy these measures flourish in profusion. At other times they are reduced in number, some, like the ell, being discarded, and others, like the hand, being retained only for some highly specialized purpose.

Now in order that a short joiner, for instance, could co-operate successfully with a tall mason, it would be necessary to standardize the measures. At the same time it would be found convenient to make them commensurable.[2] But making a large number of not very widely separated measures commensurable would automatically lead to the repeated use of rather small whole numbers. It would in fact lead quite automatically to the establishment in some degree of a pattern of proportional relationships between the measures.

It is surprising how many English measures appear in the proportional scale which we derived from the height of a man 72 inches high. This scale consists of the following measurements:

1 in.	2 in.	4 in.	8 in.
3 in.	6 in.	1 ft. 0 in.	2 ft. 0 in.
9 in.	1 ft. 6 in.	3 ft. 0 in.	6 ft. 0 in.

Of the twelve measurements, no fewer than six are also measures: the inch, the hand (4 in.), the foot, the span (9 in.), the yard and the fathom.

The fact that measures tend automatically to form proportional scales of preferred dimensions seems to be precisely what Vitruvius is trying to explain. This happens, not because the measures are derived from the human figure in the first place, though they usually are, but through the process which occurs later of standardizing them and making them commensurable.[3]

Vitruvius' own example is drawn from the Roman system of measures, which can be arranged in a similar table:

1 digit	1 palm (4 digits)	1 foot	(16 digits)
	1 cubit (24 digits)	man's height (96 digits)	

[1] III, i, 5: 'The measures, which are necessarily used in all works, are also derived from the members of the human body; as the digit, the palm, the foot, and the cubit...' (Newton's translation).

[2] But note the early use of measures related by $\sqrt{2}$, and occasionally $\sqrt{3}$. See, for instance, Berriman's *Historical Metrology* (1953), and article on 'Measures and Weights, Ancient', in the *Encyclopaedia Britannica*.

[3] Corbusier argues in *Le Modulor* (1950) that the feet-inches system is superior to the metric system because it is derived from the human figure. The view put forward here is that this is merely of historical significance, and that the feet-inches system is superior only in so far as it retains traces of a superior pattern of proportional relationships.

Here we have the beginnings of another double geometric progression. Vitruvius himself goes out of his way to point out the repetition of ratios which occurs: 'Non minus etiam, quod pes hominis altitudinis *sextam* habet partem...cubitumque animadverterunt ex *sex* palmis constare...';[1] '...relinquitur pes *quattuor* palmorum, palmus autem habet *quattuor* digitos....'[2]

There could be no clearer confirmation that in talking of proportion Vitruvius had in mind a 'real' theory and a practical system of applying it, which, whatever its details, favoured the repetition of ratios. Indeed, he seems to come closer here to a clear statement of this principle than any other writer before the end of the eighteenth century.[3]

THE PERFECT NUMBER

A further difficulty in Vitruvius' chapter on proportion is presented by the discussion of perfect numbers.[4] Here, if anywhere, 'the words are...put together in such a manner as seems to us to have no coherence or sense'.[5] Vitruvius identifies the perfect number, 'perfectus numerus', as the Latin equivalent of the Greek τέλειος.[6] Now the conception of the perfect number had had a long history among Greek mathematicians, stretching back to Pythagoras. In the course of this history it had been modified from time to time, and the definition had changed completely. Thus while 10 was a perfect number to the Pythagoreans, 6 was perfect to Euclid, but in a quite different and highly technical sense.

Vitruvius, however, seems to be quite unaware of this. He throws together numbers which are 'perfect' in quite different senses without distinguishing between them. He even goes as far as adding 10 and 6 together, and appears to assume quite arbitrarily that the result, 16, is also perfect.

The relevance of the section to the subject of the chapter as a whole is also obscure. We are told that the ancients obtained the digit, palm, foot and cubit from the human body, 'et eas distribuerunt in perfectum numerum'.[7] There is no reason, however, why we should deny to Vitruvius the right to define 'perfectus numerus' in any way he thinks fit. We have seen that he is interested in the patterns of proportional relationships between different measures, and that these patterns involve

---

[1] *De architectura* (1931), III, i, 7.   [2] *Ibid.* III, i, 8.

[3] The principle of the repetition of ratios seems to have been first clearly stated by Barca in his *Saggio sopra il bello di proporzione in architettura* (Bassano, 1806).

[4] *De architectura* (1931), III, i, 5-8.   [5] *Ibid.* (1791), I, ii, 1.

[6] *Ibid.* (1931) III, i, 5.

[7] *Ibid.* III, i, 5. None of the translations make any sense of this. Granger: 'And these they grouped into the perfect number...'. Newton: 'These are divided into the perfect number...'. Gwilt: '...these form a perfect number...'.

the repetition of certain numbers. The Greeks, for instance, used the decimal system to a great extent in their system of measures:

$$10 \text{ feet} = 1 \text{ acaina}, \quad 10 \text{ acainas} = 1 \text{ plethron}.$$

Here the pattern of proportional relationships which has developed spontaneously is the single geometric progression 1, 10, 100, and the number which is repeated and in which Vitruvius is interested is 10.

There is every reason to believe that what Vitruvius meant by a perfect number is any number which has been selected for use as the *base* of a system of numeration or of measures. In the example of measures which we have just considered, and in the decimal system of numeration, 10 is the perfect number. In duodecimal systems 12 is the perfect number, and in binary systems 2.

Euclid defined the perfect number as one which is equal to the sum of its own factors, including 1. This is a mathematical definition, and there can be no argument about whether a number is perfect according to it or not: 6 is perfect, because it is the sum of 1, 2 and 3; 28 is perfect, because it is the sum of 1, 2, 4, 7 and 14.

To Vitruvius, on the other hand, the perfect number is not a matter of mathematics at all, but a statement of *social convention*. There is thus nothing odd about the fact that the perfect number can have a history. As Vitruvius points out, 'the ancients believed the perfect number to be that which is called ten, because ten is the number of the fingers of the hands'.[1] In other words, the use of the number 10 as the base of the most common system of numeration, the decimal system, arises from man's habit of counting on his fingers.

In practice, other numbers with a greater range of factors, like 12, would have been more convenient, and were in fact often introduced in the development of systems of measures. The number 6, which happens also to be an example of Euclid's perfect numbers, occurs in the digit-palm-foot-cubit system.[2] So does the number 16,[3] which also supplanted the number 10 in the Roman system of money.[4]

If this explanation of what Vitruvius meant by a perfect number is accepted, there is very little in the chapter which remains obscure. It is not quite clear perhaps why he stresses the fact that the perfect numbers 6 and 10 add together to form the 'most perfect number' 16, but he may merely intend to amuse his readers with what is no more than a mathematical coincidence. In fact, the number 16 seems to be the least important of these numbers.

[1] *De architectura*, III, i, 5 (Newton's translation).
[2] *Ibid*. III, i, 7; height of a man = 6 feet; cubit = 6 palms.
[3] *Ibid*. III, i, 8; 1 foot = 4 palms = 16 digits. Strictly speaking 4 is the base of the system here.
[4] *Ibid*. III, i, 8; 1 denarius = 16 asses.

Finally, the statement that the ancients obtained digit, palm, foot and cubit from the human body, 'et eas distribuerunt in perfectum numerum', is now beginning to mean something. The preposition 'in', translated as 'into' by Newton and Granger, is difficult to explain. But the general sense of the passage seems to be that, in determining the pattern of proportional relationships linking these units of measurement, the ancients used certain numbers, and that numbers used in this way are what Vitruvius chooses to call 'perfect numbers'.

CONCLUSIONS

The results of this discussion can now be summarized. The statement that Vitruvius' work contains no real theory of proportion seems to be true only in the sense that the account which Vitruvius does give of proportion is neither full nor detailed, and does not appear to us at first sight very coherent. The lack of completeness and detail is explained by the fact that Vitruvius did not set out to write a specialized treatise on the theory of proportion, and in his remarks on the subject he could reasonably assume a knowledge of its general principles on the part of the reader, which we do not now possess. This goes a long way towards explaining the apparent lack of coherence as well.

It seems fairly clear that Vitruvius had in his mind a system of proportion which was both *analytical* and *commensurable*, based on the use of scales of preferred dimensions linked in patterns of proportional relationships. Once this is accepted, many of his remarks at once begin to make more sense, particularly those on the connexion between proportion, the human figure, weights and measures, and the perfect number. And we are immediately led to an extremely interesting theory of the history of proportion.

Analytical and commensurable systems in architecture were developed quite spontaneously at first, through the natural growth of systems of measures. Later, no doubt, the value of proportion became consciously understood, and systems of proportion would be detached from systems of measurement.

Vitruvius does not add that these systems of proportion would then enter into competition with the very different systems, geometrical and incommensurable, which would be developed separately in connexion with the more individual arts of pottery, painting and sculpture. After the classical period in Greece, analytical and commensurable systems became dominant. But traces of the geometrical systems survive as 'islands' in Vitruvius' work.

The attempt which has been made here to reconstruct the details of Vitruvius' own system of proportion has been of a tentative nature, limited to the following-up of one or two clues, and based in part on speculative interpretations of the words 'proportio' and 'symmetria'. It has, however, led to a real system of proportion which might conceivably be of more than historical interest.

Finally, our investigation seems to show that Vitruvius, at first sight so muddled on the subject of proportion, was in many ways far ahead of his later interpreters and commentators. For instance, although he has often been accused of doing so, he never tried to establish the false analogy between musical harmony and architectural proportion which exposed Renaissance theory to so much destructive criticism. 'Commensurability' is treated merely as a means to an end, while a mature theory of proportion, derived from the Greeks, seems to hide not very far away behind statements which appear at times to be almost incoherent.

CHAPTER III

THE THEORY OF PROPORTION
IN THE RENAISSANCE (1)

INTRODUCTION

From the time of Vitruvius to that of Alberti there is little literature referring to the problem of proportion, though enough to show that it was very much in people's minds from time to time. But from Alberti onwards the subject occupies an important place, at first in the theory of architecture and the arts subordinate to it, and later in the growing theory of aesthetics and criticism in general.

Unfortunately, we cannot record a steady progress in the theory of proportion and the theory of architecture of which it formed part comparable to that which took place in the natural sciences. For Leonardo there had been no gulf dividing art from science, both of which were governed by experience.[1] But the spirit of free inquiry based on experiment, which he represents, disappeared in Italy before Alberti's ideas had been properly explored; it was replaced by reliance on the authority of Vitruvius, whose ideas on the subject of proportion are, as we have just seen, obscure and difficult to interpret. As a result, the theory of proportion which France, and later England, received from Italy is confusing and inconsistent, and raised more questions than it answered. So instead of progress, we find a constant revival of the same arguments, now in one country and now in another, over a period of three hundred and fifty years, until in the nineteenth century what remained of the Renaissance theory of proportion shared in the collapse of the theory of architecture as a whole.

In spite of this, the history of the discussion is well worth examining. A number of important principles emerge, and the study of what can be regarded as the unsuccessful Renaissance experiment in proportion is full of lessons for us today. The ground to be covered includes that on which Professor Wittkower has thrown so much light in his *Architectural Principles in the Age of Humanism*. However, we shall go over it again, not merely for the sake of completeness, or of investigating one or two additional details, but to assess the theory of proportion from our own point of view today.

[1] E.g. '...sound rules are the daughters of sound experience, the common mother of all the sciences and arts'; *Selections from the Notebooks of Leonardo da Vinci*, edited by Irma A. Richter (1952), p. 224.

Professor Wittkower is primarily interested in presenting the theory of proportion as an example of the wider neo-Platonist philosophy of the Renaissance.
From this point of view the interesting thing, for instance, about the eighteenth-
century critics is their failure to understand this philosophy.[1] Here, however, we
are more concerned with the theory of proportion itself, and besides reporting
these critics we shall enter into the debate.

SOURCES OF RENAISSANCE THEORY

The main source of the Renaissance theory of proportion, and, indeed, of the
theory of architecture as a whole, was, of course, Vitruvius, whose work was rediscovered in the fifteenth century. The first edition was that of Sulpitius, published
in Rome in 1486, but it had circulated in manuscript form considerably earlier,
just as Alberti's *De re aedificatoria* had, which was first printed posthumously in 1485,
and which owes much to Vitruvius, although Alberti's own attitude towards him is
highly critical compared to that of later writers.

It would be unfair to say that the Renaissance owes to Vitruvius a tradition of
muddled thinking about architecture, although some writers do owe their confusion to
his obscurity. It is, however, tempting to wonder whether the Renaissance might not
have got farther with the problem of proportion if theorists had had to make a fresh
start with it, as they did in the case of perspective. As it was, they got from Vitruvius
a partly unintelligible theory, and a variety of apparently unrelated practical hints,
which were handed on from one writer to the next for what they were worth.

But from Vitruvius came the basic ideas of the importance of proportion as a
source of beauty,[2] of its being concerned with the relationship of the parts to each
other and to the whole,[3] and of its being subject to reason and rules rather than to
intuition.[4] His most important contribution to the practice of proportion is the

---

[1] E.g. of Lord Kames: '...he too was unaware of the deeper bond that for a Renaissance mind united
ratios in music and visible objects' (*Architectural Principles in the Age of Humanism*, 2nd ed. 1952, p. 133).

[2] 'Haec autem ita fieri debent, ut habeatur ratio firmitatis, utilitatis, venustatis.... Venustatis vero, cum
fuerit operis species grata et elegans membrorumque commensus iustas habeat symmetriarum ratiocinationes.'
'All these ought to be constructed with strength, utility and beauty.... Beauty, when the form of the work is
agreeable and elegant, and the proportions of the members are correspondent to the rules of symmetry'
(I, iii, 2; Newton's transl.).

[3] 'Item symmetria est ex ipsius operis membris conveniens consensus ex partibusque separatis ad universae
figurae speciem ratae partis responsus.' 'Symmetry is also the proper agreement of the same members of
a work, and the proportional correspondence of the separate parts to the form of the whole object' (I, ii, 4;
Newton's transl.).

[4] 'Aedium compositio constat ex symmetria, cuius rationem diligentissime architecti tenere debent. Ea
autem paritur a proportione, quae graece *analogia* dicitur.' 'The composition of temples is governed by the
laws of symmetry, which an architect ought well to understand; this arises from proportion, which is called
by the Greeks, *analogia*' (III, i, 1; Newton's transl.).

use of the harmonic scale, by means of which the leading dimensions are made sub-multiples of the whole. His unrelated practical hints include a great mass of rules for the proportions of the orders, of temples, and of courtyards and rooms of houses, although there is admittedly little system to be found among them, and they are based not only on the use of commensurable dimensions, but also occasionally on the use of the $\sqrt{2}$ rectangle as well. Finally, the Renaissance owes to Vitruvius, or perhaps to a misunderstanding of him, its obsession with the analogy between the human figure and architecture.[1]

Within a few years of the first edition of Vitruvius, a number of other important works were published for the first time. In 1482 Ficino completed his translation of Plato. In the same year the first printed edition appeared of Campanus' four-teenth-century translation of Euclid from Arabic into Latin. Ten years later the first printed edition of Boethius' works was published at Venice.

The importance of Euclid in any mathematical study of proportion is too obvious to require illustration. It is interesting to notice that during the Middle Ages Plato was thought of as a contemporary of Euclid, and the mistake was not finally cleared up until the publication of Commandinus' translation of Euclid from the Greek in 1572. This may have led Renaissance theorists to regard Plato as a reliable interpreter of the mature Greek theory of mathematical proportion. In fact, during Plato's lifetime this was only being developed in the form which is later found in Euclid's 'Elements' by Eudoxus, who worked out the application of the mathematical theory of proportion to incommensurable quantities.[2]

Professor Wittkower stresses the importance of neo-Platonism in the Renaissance theory of architecture, and points out how the application of musical proportions to architecture was suggested by the way in which Plato applied them to cosmology in the *Timaeus*.[3] There is, however, no evidence to suggest that the Greeks themselves ever used this type of proportion in architecture, and the idea that Plato has more than an accidental importance in the technical theory of architectural proportion has little to recommend it. His importance in the history of aesthetics is of course quite another matter.

Boethius had been important throughout the Middle Ages and his work on arithmetic and music—based on the Greek theory expounded by Nicomachus, whose *Introductio arithmetica* Boethius had translated into Latin—had been used as

---

[1] 'Namque non potest aedis ulla sine symmetria atque proportione rationem habere compositionis, nisi uti ad hominis bene figurati membrorum habuerit exactam rationem.' 'For a building cannot be well composed without the rules of symmetry and proportion; nor unless the members, as in a well formed human body, have a perfect agreement' (III, i, 1; Newton's transl.).

[2] See Heath's *A History of Greek Mathematics* (1921), vol. I, p. 326.

[3] *Architectural Principles in the Age of Humanism* (2nd ed.), pp. 91–2.

text-books. In them he explains the application of numerical proportion to musical harmony. Accordingly Renaissance architects who wished to act on Vitruvius' advice to study music would naturally turn to Boethius. But there is every reason to believe that the use they made of what they found there was completely novel, and would have astonished Vitruvius, whose interest in music arose, not from the possibility of applying the theory of musical harmony to the problem of architectural proportion, but simply from the importance of acoustics in the design of theatres. The myth which identifies Vitruvius with the 'musical' theory of architectural proportion seems to have originated in the sixteenth century,[1] and has continued up to the present day.

Alberti's method of the 'generation of ratios', which will require detailed discussion, goes back through Boethius to Nichomachus.[2] It is also a fact of very great interest that Nicomachus studied certain double geometric progressions[3] including the progression

$$
\begin{array}{llllll}
1 & 2 & 4 & 8 & 16 & \ldots \\
 & 3 & 6 & 12 & 24 & \ldots \\
 & & 9 & 18 & 36 & \ldots \\
 & & & 27 & 54 & \ldots \\
 & & & & 81 & \ldots
\end{array}
$$

This has important applications in the study of musical harmony, in the interpretation of Plato's cosmology,[4] and in the understanding of the Renaissance 'musical' theory of proportion.

Mathematically it is a shortcoming of Nicomachus that he deals always with particular cases rather than with general principles, but it is a little difficult to see how the double geometric progression could be discussed in general terms without the use of algebraic notation. Even Euclid only touches on some of its properties indirectly.[5]

The sources of Renaissance theory were not of course confined to Greece and Rome, but what was owed to the more recent though less articulate past is more difficult to trace. A clue can be found in the work of Cennino Cennini, who represents the Byzantine tradition.[6] Cennini expresses the proportions of the human figure in terms of the face,[7] unlike Vitruvius, who expresses them in terms of the

---

[1] Alberti does not make this mistake, which probably originated when it became more important to give every theory the authority of Vitruvius. E.g. 'Hoc fuit Vitruvii consilium in aedibus et earum partibus ab auribus ad oculos traducere rationem' ('This was the advice of Vitruvius, in buildings and their parts to transfer the system from the ears to the eyes'); Jerome Cardan, *De subtilitate*, book XIII, p. 494.

[2] *Introduction to Arithmetic* (transl. M. L. d'Ooge, 1926), II, v and xxvi.

[3] *Ibid.* II, iii and iv.   [4] *Ibid.* II, ii.

[5] 'Elements', book VIII, propositions 9–13.

[6] *Il libro dell'arte.*   [7] *Ibid.* chapters xxx and lxx.

height of the whole figure. Cennini is followed by many of the Renaissance writers on the subject, who, whether they determined human proportions empirically or according to a mathematical system, often used the 'face' or 'head' as a module. This may have also led them to give greater importance to the use of a module in architecture than Vitruvius does.

But much of the medieval heritage was rejected in favour of classical learning, which is one reason why Gothic principles of design are so difficult to recover. There is little doubt that these principles were geometrical, while the Renaissance returned to an analytical system of proportion.

PROPORTION IN GENERAL

(A) AESTHETIC PRINCIPLES

The scientific study of proportion as a source of beauty, and the attempt to formulate rules for its control, is only undertaken against a background of certain aesthetic principles. The most general of these is the principle that art is concerned with creating things which are beautiful. This has always been taken for granted in practice by artists and craftsmen, and until recently[1] in theory by philosophers, whose arguments have been concerned not with the value of beauty, but with its nature. Alberti had no doubts at all that architecture was very much concerned with beauty, and he comes back to the subject again and again.[2]

The second principle is that objective standards of beauty are possible, and that our sense of beauty is not entirely arbitrary and unpredictable, but is aroused by certain real qualities in external objects which we can learn to understand and reproduce. Now here there is plenty of room for argument between those who stress the objective aspect of beauty, and the possibility of formulating rules of art, and those who stress the subjective side of our judgment of beauty, and fall back on intuition unaided by reason. Of the latter Alberti had this to say: 'There are some who will by no means allow of this, and say that men are guided by a variety of opinions in their judgment of beauty and of buildings; and that the forms of structures must vary according to every man's particular taste and fancy, and not be tied down to any rules of art. A common thing with the ignorant, to despise what they do not understand. . . .'[3]

---

[1] Beauty was thrown out of the front door of aesthetics by R. G. Collingwood in his *Principles of Art* (1938), but Allsopp in his application of Collingwood's theory to architecture seems to let it in at the back door. When he speaks of such factors as shape, texture, colour, pattern, rhythm, balance, unity, space, etc., as stimuli to the emotions which the architect is concerned to express (*Art and the Nature of Architecture*, 1952, p. 24), he is simply making a list of qualities in objects which stimulate our sense of beauty.

[2] *Ten Books on Architecture* (1955), especially I, ix; VI, ii, iv; IX, v.   [3] *Ibid.* p. 113.

If this principle is accepted, a science of beauty becomes possible, and a science of art, of which the science of proportion forms a part. Michel maintains that Alberti founded this science, and explains how it differs from the traditional lore worked out by trial and error and handed down from generation to generation, which is represented in the work of Alberti's predecessor Cennini.[1] The scientific approach to art flourished in the Renaissance in the work of many others besides Alberti, but as we shall see it began to decline in Italy in the sixteenth century.

But to establish that certain qualities of external objects do stimulate our sense of beauty, however much this may also be affected by subjective factors in our own minds, is not in itself enough. It is also necessary to show that proportion is itself one of these qualities, and to explain why this is so in terms of a consistent theory. While various attempts were made to do this, it remains one of the weakest sides of the Renaissance theory of art. As we shall see, the theory of proportion was seriously criticized by Perrault in the seventeenth century, and finally destroyed by British critics in the eighteenth century, long before the wider aspects of Renaissance theory were rejected.

In the early Renaissance there were, however, no doubts that proportion was one of the objective causes of beauty. The need for a rational explanation of this was not so strong at a time when architects were experimenting with forms which were in fact new to their eyes, even though they were taken from the ruins of Rome and the writings of Vitruvius. The designer, especially the designer who is using abstract or unfamiliar forms, knows always from his own experience that certain relationships of shapes are more pleasing to the eye than others, not merely through association or because of their fitness for their purpose, but in themselves.

The fact was keenly realized in the Renaissance, and writers repeatedly drew attention to it. Alberti gives the classic definition: 'I shall define Beauty to be a harmony of all the parts in whatsoever subject it appears, fitted together with such proportion and connexion that nothing could be added, diminished or altered, but for the worse....'[2] Leonardo, in comparing painting with poetry, tells the poet that 'in my opinion your invention is much inferior to the painter's, for the sole reason that there is no composition of harmonious proportions' ('proportionalità armonica') and he continues with a eulogy of 'divine proportion' ('diuina proportione').[3] Barbaro speaks of the 'power, the necessity, and finally the utility of proportion', without which nothing can be produced of 'pleasure or delight'.[4]

[1] Paul-Henri Michel, *La Pensée de L. B. Alberti* (1930), pp. 334–41.
[2] *Ten Books on Architecture*, p. 113.
[3] *Paragone*, p. 68 (Irma A. Richter's transl., 1949 ed.). 'Divine proportion' seems to be used here in a general sense, and without the connexion with the golden section which it is sometimes supposed to have had. [4] Footnote to Barbaro's edition of Vitruvius, 1567, p. 80.

The nearest that the Renaissance got to a theory explaining the facts of proportion was the 'musical' theory with which Professor Wittkower deals[1] and which Alberti himself originated.[2] It does not, however, explain all the facts of proportion as it was practised in the Renaissance, and Alberti made no claim that it did.[3] So before we discuss this theory, a more general outline of the Renaissance practice of proportion will be given.

(B) HARMONIC AND ARITHMETIC SCALES

The Renaissance inherited from Vitruvius what we have described as the harmonic scale. By means of this the dimensions of the parts are expressed as submultiples of the dimensions of the whole, or of larger parts. We have seen that in certain conditions this does in fact constitute a system of proportion. This system was more important in the early Renaissance.

Alberti expresses not merely the proportions of the orders in this way, but he systematically works out the proportions of whole buildings.[4] Furthermore, he seems to be clearly aware of the possible relationship between the use of the harmonic scale and the generation of geometric progressions. In describing the proportions of the Doric base,[5] he deliberately stresses this: 'Thus the height of the whole base was three times that of the die, and the breadth of the die was three times the height of the base.' Here we have the first three terms of the progression 1, 3, 9, 27, ... which is constantly appearing in the literature of the subject, and which owes its importance to the use which Plato made of it in the *Timaeus*.[6] It also appears in the proportions of one of Alberti's versions of the Doric capital, but here he draws no attention to it.[7] But in general Alberti's use of the harmonic scale, like that of Vitruvius, is not nearly simple enough to yield anything very systematic in the way of the repetition of ratios.

The characteristic feature of the system is that the dimensions of the smaller parts, down to the most minute details of the orders, are obtained from those of the larger parts by successive subdivisions. It was used by Serlio,[8] from whom it

---

[1] *Architectural Principles in the Age of Humanism*, part IV.

[2] *Ten Books on Architecture*, pp. 196 ff.

[3] *Ibid.* p. 199; 'There are some other natural proportions for the use of structures, which are not borrowed from numbers, but from the roots and powers of squares....'

[4] Note especially the illustrations to the chapter on basilicas, *Ten Books on Architecture*, VII, xiv.

[5] *Ten Books on Architecture*, p. 142.

[6] See Francesco Giorgi's 'Memorandum for S. Francesco della Vigna', reproduced by Professor Wittkower as an appendix to his *Architectural Principles in the Age of Humanism*.

[7] *Ten Books on Architecture*, p. 144.

[8] *Libro primo d'architettura* (1560–2), translated by Peake, 1611.

was borrowed by John Shute.[1] Gradually, however, it gave way to the use of an arithmetic scale, which relies on multiplication rather than division, and by means of which the dimensions of details of the orders, for instance, are expressed as multiples of minutes. After a period of experiment, Palladio's method of dividing the diameter of the base of the column into 60 minutes prevailed.

Vincente Scamozzi, in discussing the advantages of the 60-minute module,[2] almost stumbles on the principle of a proportional system based on factors. Of the number 60 he remarks: 'il contient en soi 10 divisions entières: comme le 2, 3, 4, 5, et 6 de petits nombres, qui est de même que de dire 1/30, 1/20, 1/15, 1/12, 1/10, et depuis 10, 12, 15, 20 et 30 de nombres plus grands, qui désignent, 1/6, 1/5, 1/4, 1/3 et 1/2.' He has worked out for us here the triple geometric progression:

1	2	4	or	1/60	1/30	1/15
3	6	12		1/20	1/10	1/5
5	10	20		1/12	1/6	1/3
15	30	60		1/4	1/2	1

but he is in fact probably only concerned with indicating the general usefulness of a sexagesimal system of numeration. He goes on to say that 'on peut encore diviser le Module autrement comme en 1/7, 1/8, 1/9 partie, et autres semblables. Vitruve s'est encore servi de cette manière de mesurer, lorsqu'il a traité des Mesures des Entablements; mais ces sortes de divisions sont difficiles à entendre.'

The reason why the Vitruvian system was replaced by the use of the arithmetic scale of modules and minutes is given by Perrault: 'This way was left off by the moderns for no other reason, but because they found that they could not accommodate it to the irregular measures that are in the members of the noble remains of antiquity, which are found very different from what Vitruvius hath left us: so that they would have been obliged to alter them in some measure, to reduce them to the regular proportions which this method requires.'[3] Again, 'what has obliged the moderns to make use of the same minutes, is the necessity they often had to denote measures that held no proportion'.[4] Perrault paradoxically advocated a return to the Vitruvian system purely on grounds of convenience, as he opposed the idea that proportion itself had any aesthetic value.[5]

Thus the early Renaissance used a system of describing the proportions of the

---

[1] *The First and Chief Groundes of Architecture* (1563; facsimile edition 1912).

[2] *Idea dell'architettura universale* (1615), translated by A. C. d'Aviler in the French edition of Scamozzi's works (1713), p. 120.

[3] Claude Perrault, *Ordonnance des cinq espèces de colonnes* (1683), translated by John James under the title *A Treatise of the Five Orders in Architecture* (1722), p. xiv.

[4] *Ibid.* p. 5.   [5] See Plate 1.

I. CORINTHIAN ORDER FROM PERRAULT'S 'FIVE ORDERS OF
COLUMNS IN ARCHITECTURE'

Harmonic subdivisions adopted purely for convenience.

orders which contained at least the germ of a system of proportion. The later Renaissance abandoned this system in favour of a purely empirical system. The use of minutes was an accurate way either of measuring the works of antiquity, or of recording particularly pleasing proportions arrived at by trial and error.[1]

(C) THE HUMAN FIGURE

An interesting parallel can be found between the methods of determining the proportions of the orders and those of the human figure. A close relationship was supposed to exist between the two by Vitruvius, and this was stressed throughout the Renaissance. It is therefore worth studying in some detail.

Many writers regarded the study of human proportions purely as an exercise in proportional theory, which need not be taken too seriously in actual painting or sculpture. Thus Vasari, besides quoting Michelangelo's famous remark about the artist having his compasses in his eyes, also insists in his own study of human proportion that 'the eye must give the final judgment' and 'must decide where to take away and where to add, as it sees defect in the work...'.[2] Leonardo, even in the illustrations to his notes on human proportions, does not bother to draw with mathematical accuracy.[3] This point of view is one which we may well adopt here.

Human proportions were expressed by Renaissance writers either as submultiples of the whole height or of the face, following Vitruvius,[4] or else as multiples of a small division of the height. Usually the first, or harmonic, system was used by those seeking to develop an abstract mathematical canon of proportion, while, as in the case of the orders, the second, or arithmetical, system was found convenient by those whose approach to the subject was more empirical. Thus Gaurico,[5] Vasari and Leonardo preferred the first system while Alberti adopted the second.

In his work on painting, Alberti used the head as a module,[6] but in dealing with sculpture he used the foot.[7] This he made one-sixth of the total height of the figure, and he divided it into ten parts, which were again each subdivided into ten. There were thus 600 of the smallest units of length in the total height, and with these it was possible to give empirically determined proportions with great accuracy.

---

[1] See Plate 2.

[2] Vasari, *On Technique*, originally published as part of the *Lives*, 1550; translated by L. S. Maclehose, and edited by Professor G. Baldwin Brown (London 1907), p. 146.

[3] *Literary Works of Leonardo da Vinci*, edited by Dr J. P. Richter (Oxford, 1939), p. 244.

[4] The use of the face as a module is not stressed by Vitruvius, and it seems to spring from the Byzantine tradition represented by Cennini. See Plate 3.

[5] Pomponio Gaurico, *De sculptura*, 1504. Later included in de Laet's edition of Vitruvius (Amsterdam, 1649). [6] *De pictura* (1435).

[7] *De statua* (before 1435). A translation appears in the 1663 edition of Chambray's *Parallel*, made by Evelyn.

Of the Portico of the Rotunda

2. CORINTHIAN ORDER FROM CHAMBRAY'S 'PARALLEL'

The module is subdivided into minutes to record the results of archaeological research.

Alberti himself listed a set of proportions arrived at by taking the average of a number of admired examples.

An interesting case is that of Dürer, whose approach was also empirical, and who set out to discover the 'normal' proportions of different types of human figure by measuring numerous examples. Dürer had no time for those who tried to improve on nature by inventing artificial canons of proportion: 'If the best parts, chosen from many well-formed men, are united in one figure, it will be worthy of praise. But some are of another opinion, and discuss how men *ought* to be made.... I hold that the perfection of form and beauty is contained in the sum of all men. That man will I rather follow, who can extract this perfection aright, than one who invents some new body of proportions not to be found among men.'[1]

Dürer tried out both the harmonic and arithmetic scales. The first he used in his first book of human proportions, perhaps out of deference to Vitruvius, and he showed a diagram of the harmonic scale or 'regula' which he used.[2] But in trying to express proportions arrived at empirically by means of the harmonic scale he encountered serious difficulties.

He overcame these to some extent by the use of proportions such as $1/10 + 1/11$, but he found the second system, which he used in his later books, much more suitable for his purpose. The arithmetic scale he used was similar to Alberti's, but he divided the smallest unit of measurement still further into three parts. These, however, were rarely used.[3]

The one example of mathematical proportion and the repetition of ratios which Dürer claimed to have discovered in his researches was that of the dimensions neck-hip, hip-knee and knee-ankle. He believed that these ought to form a geometric progression: 'Now I come to the three dimensions. I find that they agree amongst themselves in a certain proportion, so that the proportion which the length of the body makes with the length of the hip, taken from the top of the thigh to the middle of the knee, is the same as the proportion which the latter makes with the shin.'[4]

Another interesting case is that of Cardan, who modified and extended the proportions of the human figure given by Vitruvius. Barbaro reproduced Cardan's

---

[1] *Literary Remains of A. Dürer*, ed. W. M. Conway (Cambridge, 1889), p. 250. The quotation is from the British Museum MS. vol. IV, 37. Hogarth clearly did Dürer a serious injustice in including him among the authors who 'assure you that this curious method of measuring *will produce beauty far beyond any nature doth afford*...'; *Analysis of Beauty* (1753), p. 91 in the edition of 1955.

[2] *De symmetria partium in rectis formis humanorum corporum* (Nuremberg, 1532); translated from the German edition of 1528, book I. See Plates 4–6.

[3] *Ibid.* book II.

[4] *Ibid.* book I. The Latin reads: 'Nunc ad illas tres mensiones redeo, eas scito inter se certa proportione convenire oportere, sic ut qua proportione corporis longitudo congruat cum longitudine coxae, ducta ratione a summo femore ad genu medium, ea proportione haec cum tibia comparetur.'

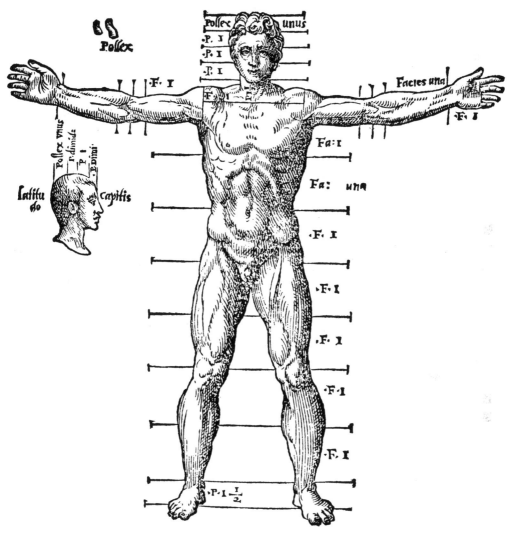

3. HUMAN FIGURE FROM BARBARO'S 'VITRUVIUS'

The face is used as a module.

45

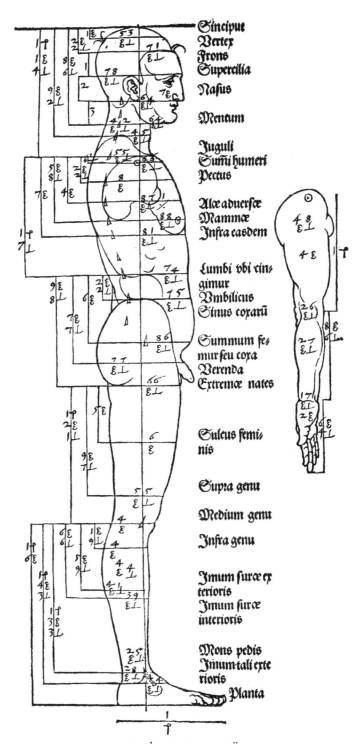

4. MAN'S FIGURE BY DÜRER

Dürer's use of the 'arithmetic' scale.

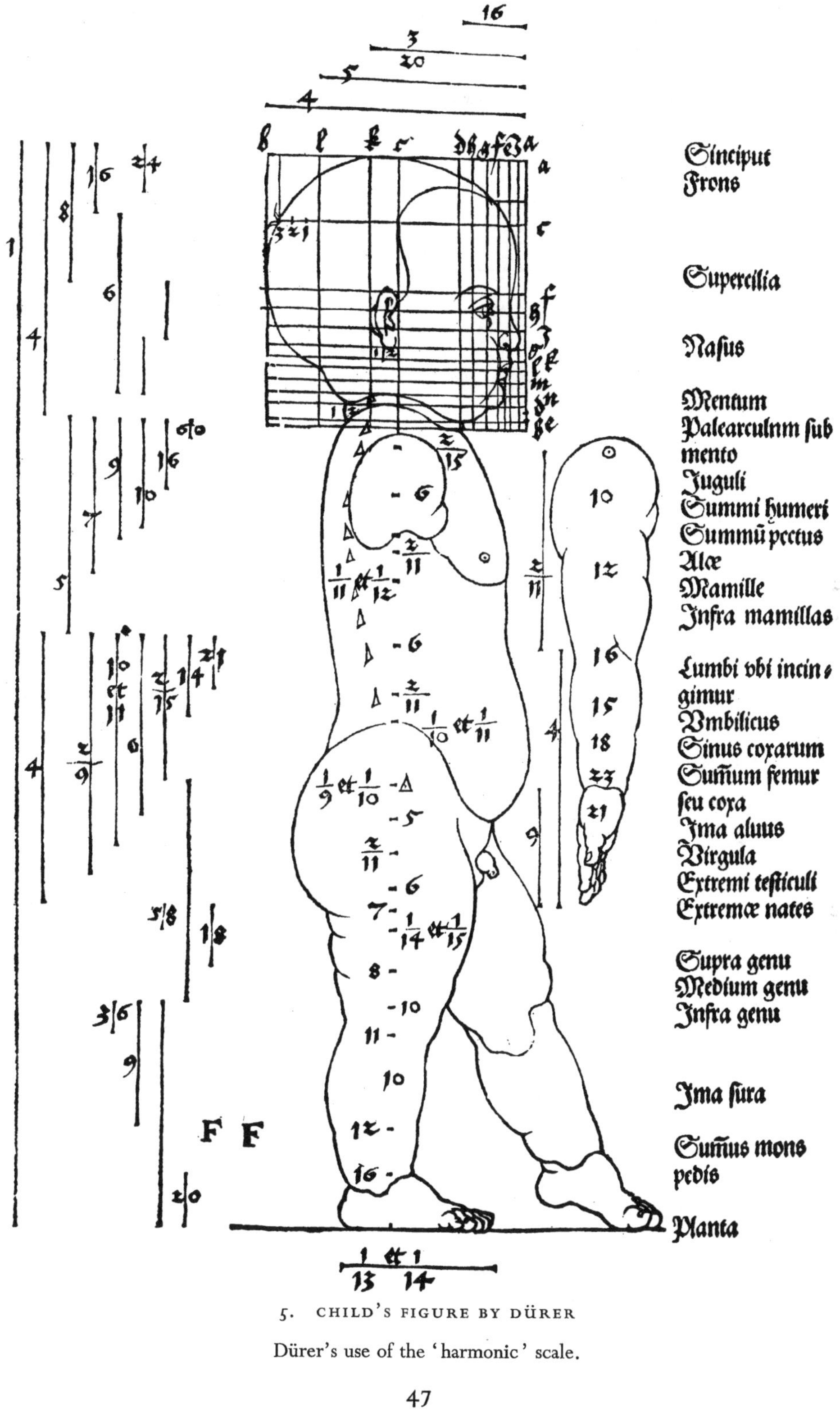
Sinciput
Frons
Supercilia
Nasus
Mentum
Palearculnm sub mento
Juguli
Summi humeri
Summū pectus
Alæ
Mamille
Infra mamillas
Lumbi vbi incin-gimur
Vmbilicus
Sinus coxarum
Sumum femur seu coxa
Ima aluus
Virgula
Extremi testiculi
Extremæ nates
Supra genu
Medium genu
Infra genu
Ima sura
Sumus mons pedis
Planta
F F

5. CHILD'S FIGURE BY DÜRER

Dürer's use of the 'harmonic' scale.

proportions in his edition of Vitruvius, making it clear that they were, like those of Vitruvius himself, based on submultiples of the total height. They were, however, expressed by Cardan himself as multiples of a small part, of which there were 180 to the total height. The result of combining harmonic and arithmetic progressions in this way is, as we have already seen, the formation of a proportional scale, based in this case on a triple geometric progression.

Cardan's proportions, which form rather an incomplete progression, are as follows:[1]

$$
\begin{array}{ccc}
1 & 2 & 4 \\
6 & 12 & 24 \\
18 & 36 & \\
30 & & \\
& 180 & \\
\end{array}
$$

Barbaro reproduces these, and also gives them as submultiples of the total height:[2]

$$
\begin{array}{ccc}
1/180 & 1/90 & 1/45 \\
1/30 & 1/15 & 1/7\frac{1}{2} \\
1/10 & 1/5 & \\
1/6 & & \\
& 1 & \\
\end{array}
$$

Apart from hints which were perhaps given by Vitruvius, this method of proportion seems to be unique and of considerable interest.

Cardan followed Vitruvius in making the face a tenth part of the total height, but others, like Vasari and Gaurico, preferred to make it a ninth part.[3] It is easy to see why this was done when we find that Gaurico subdivided the face itself into three equal parts. In this way he obtained the three terms 1, 3, 27, of the progression 1, 3, 9, 27, ..., to which so much importance was attached. Leonardo completed this progression in one of his experiments in human proportion, by making the total height equal to three braccias, and the face equal to a third of a braccia.[4] Thus:

Total height = 3 braccias = 9 faces = 27 subdivisions.

Leonardo's notes on proportion are of the greatest interest and variety. In one of the most interesting passages he applies the harmonic system to the human face,[5] in exactly the way in which Vitruvius applied it to the Attic base, using only very

[1] De subtilitate (1559), book XI, pp. 462–3.   [2] De architectura (1567), p. 89.

[3] 'Sed age, hominem, longe aliter quam Architectus, vivum stantemque dimetiamur, scilicet in novem de longitudine portiones'; Gaurico, De sculptura (1504).

[4] The Literary Works of Leonardo da Vinci (1939), vol. I, p. 245.

[5] Ibid. vol. I, pp. 245–6.

Alberti Dureri clariss: pictoris et Geometræ de Symmetria liber primus.

Depicturus humanam effigiem, hanc rationē sequitor. In pposi-
tam regulam quæ effigiem quam facere vis longitudine sua excedat,
lineam ducito, eius cuius picturam esse placuit altitudinis. Sic vt lineæ
prim⁹ punctus verticem, extremus calcem describat, proque diuersitate
formarum, vt illas longas aut breues in animo cōcepisti, singulis suas
lineas accommodato, easdemqȝ singulatim partitor. Quare quoties-
cunqȝ in sequentibus partium numeros audies, eos petendos scias, ex
statura totius altitudinis a vertice ad calcem vsqȝ ei⁹ cuius effigies insti-
tuta sit, cuius vnica illa linea diligentia summa distinguenda est, quæ
distinctio perueniat a duab⁹ partibus ad partes aut quinquaginta, aut
centum aut quotcunqȝ tandem partib: vsus sit. Eas partes omnes suis
numeris notatas ad illam longam in regula ductam lineam referes,
sic vt cum eius primo siue initiali puncto consentiant, deinceps vero pro
sua quæqȝ diuersitate discrepent, vt necesse est. Atqȝ hac via paucionb⁹
numeris longiores partes notabuntur et contra pluribus breuiores. fiet
autem de tota lōgitudine, dimidium lineæ. 2. pars tertia. 3. pars quarta
4. atqȝ ita consequenter. Quas etiam ipsas hoc modo notatas partes si
res poposcerit vlterius pro tuo arbitrio, dimidiato in alios siue pares siue
impares numeros Nam qui aliqȝ rem accurate metiri cupit, dum vna
certa partitione comprehendere omnia nequit, necessitate ad partium
cōminutionem defertur. Quod a me factum postea apparebit sepe enim
duplices, sepe triplices numeros collocatos videbis / magnos / medios /
pares / impares, qbus prox: ad veritatem rei pertingere posse visus sum
Cœterum numerorum eorum qui a me designati sunt, compositio,
mutari et pro alterius ingenio aliter vsurpari poterit, Vt autem omnia
quæ et dicta hactenus a nobis sunt et postea dicentur melius intelligan-
tur, Illam regulam cum suis partib: et partium notis quomodo facere
docui hic appingam. ante enim omnia huius rectitudinem cōstare opor-
tet absqȝ quo immensus labor et temporis iufinitas, vix omnium partium nominatas lōgitudines in totius longitudinis statura a vertice ad
calcem vsqȝ perquesitura videatur.

6. DÜRER'S 'REGULA'

The 'harmonic' scale used by Dürer.

simple submultiples. The result is a pattern of proportional relationships given by precisely the same geometric progression:

$$
\begin{array}{cccc}
 & & & 3/4 \\
 & 1 & 1/2 & 1/4 \\
2/3 & 1/3 & 1/6 & 1/12
\end{array}
$$

Leonardo's work on proportion would repay very much more investigation, but enough has been said on the proportions of the human figure for our present purpose.

A general picture has begun to emerge of a great wealth and freedom of experiment, and of the value of the human figure as a field for this kind of research. The problem of proportion was attacked from two different sides. Alberti and Dürer were interested in measuring the actual human figure, just as architects were beginning to measure examples of the orders surviving from antiquity. Cardan and Leonardo experimented with mathematical systems of proportion whose utility could be tested out in the difficult task of fitting them to the human figure. From our point of view the most interesting thing is the way in which patterns of proportional relationships and geometric progressions were developed in the course of these experiments, sometimes spontaneously and sometimes, like the 1, 3, 9, 27, ... progression, deliberately.

The last two sections have dealt with methods of proportion which were analytical (in the sense that the problem of proportion is reduced to one dimension) and commensurable. Far simpler commensurability is usually produced by the harmonic scale than by the arithmetic scale, but even so it is rarely very simple. But before we go on to discuss methods of restricting proportion to the simplest possible commensurability, that of the musical consonances, a word must be added about the use of incommensurable proportions in the Renaissance.

(D) INCOMMENSURABLE PROPORTIONS

(i) *The square root of two.* Vitruvius had advocated the use of the $\sqrt{2}$ rectangle, or rectangle in which the longer side is equal to the diagonal of the square on the shorter side, both for details of the orders,[1] and as a suitable shape for the atrium of a house.[2] It is no doubt for this reason that the $\sqrt{2}$ rectangle turns up from time to time in the Renaissance. Thus Shute, whose authorities are Vitruvius and Serlio, gives it an important part to play in fixing the proportions of the pedestals to the orders.[3] Palladio includes the $\sqrt{2}$ rectangle in the list of seven shapes which he recommends for the plans of rooms.[4]

[1] *De architectura*, IV, i, II.   [2] *Ibid.* VI, iii, 3.
[3] John Shute, *The First and Chief Groundes of Architecture*.
[4] Palladio, *I quattro libri dell'architettura* (transl. by Ware, *The Four Books of Architecture*), I, xxi.

This occurrence of the $\sqrt{2}$ rectangle is embarrassing if we are trying to attribute to the Renaissance a consistent theory based wholly on commensurable proportions. Legh, a nineteenth-century supporter of commensurability, tries to explain the occurrence of the square root of two in Vitruvius as an approximation to the simply commensurable ratio $7:5$.[1] Professor Wittkower suggests that 'it is probably true to say that neither Palladio nor any other Renaissance architect ever in practice used irrational proportions...'.[2]

On the other hand, we have Alberti's statement that 'there are some other natural proportions for the use of structures, which are not borrowed from numbers, but from the roots and powers of squares...',[3] and Pacioli speaks clearly of cases 'when one cannot make use of the simple symmetries like $1:2$, $1:3$, $3:4$, $2:3$, etc., but has to use the irrational proportions...'.[4] The explanation of this contradiction seems to lie in the fact that the Renaissance never really produced a consistent theory of proportion. It might have done so if the critical and experimental attitude of the fifteenth century had continued throughout the sixteenth century in Italy, but it faded out before the recommendations of Vitruvius and the results of experiment had been digested sufficiently to produce a unified theory. All that survived was on the one hand the uncritical acceptance of the authority of Vitruvius, and on the other hand a rather narrow doctrine of commensurable proportions. The latter originated with Alberti, who did not, however, himself claim that it was a complete solution to the problem.

Before leaving the $\sqrt{2}$ rectangle, it may be mentioned that $\sqrt{2}$ proportions, and the geometrical progression 1, $\sqrt{2}$, 2, $2\sqrt{2}$, ... in particular, are developed by the sort of patterns of expanding squares and circles which are illustrated by Vincente Scamozzi in the section of his work dealing with geometry.[5] Square and circle geometry of this sort played a part in the design of the centrally planned churches of the Renaissance, and the interest in it no doubt originated in Vitruvius' vague reference to the square and circle in connexion with human proportions,[6] as well as in the treatment of this kind of geometry by Plato.[7]

The θ progression, 1, θ, θ^2, ..., also develops out of square and circle geometry, and it is generated directly by a series of expanding eight-pointed stars in a similar way to that in which the ϕ progression is generated by a series of expanding pentagrams.[8] There is no direct evidence that pentagrams have ever been used in this way

---

[1] P. Legh, *Music of the Eye* (1831), p. 103.

[2] *Architectural Principles in the Age of Humanism* (2nd ed.), p. 95.

[3] *Ten Books on Architecture*, p. 199. Examples in the chapter include $\sqrt{3}$ as well as $\sqrt{2}$.

[4] *Divina proportione* (1509), quoted by Ghyka in 'Gothic canons of architecture' in the *Burlington Magazine* (March 1945), p. 74.   [5] *Oeuvres d'architecture* (French ed. of 1713), p. 2.

[6] *Architectural Principles in the Age of Humanism*, part I.   [7] *Meno*, 82 B–85 B.   [8] See p. 140 below.

in design,[1] but there is no doubt at all about the use of the eight-pointed star. It sometimes occurs structurally in architecture as the projection in plan of a system of vaulting or binding arches supporting a cupola,[2] and its possibilities as an instrument of design were firmly grasped by Leonardo. His numerous designs for centrally planned churches were nearly all based on systems of expanding eight-pointed stars, and their proportions are therefore determined by the θ series.[3]

(ii) *The golden section.* The golden section would scarcely need to be mentioned in a discussion of Renaissance proportional theory, but recently the impression has been gaining ground that it was understood and made use of at this time. Professor Ghyka, for instance, tells us that for the proportions of rooms Palladio 'seems to favour a R.A.P.' (rectangular parallelepiped) 'of characteristics 1, $\sqrt{\phi}$, ϕ, the floor and ceiling being ϕ rectangles'.[4] This is presumably a reference to the fact that Palladio includes in his list of seven favoured ratios for the sides of rooms the ratio $5:3$, a very inaccurate approximation to the ratio $\phi:1$, and that also, of the three different methods which he gives for determining the heights of rooms, one is by using the geometric mean.

Professor Wittkower's explanation of the ratio $5:3$ as the equivalent of the major sixth in music, a consonance which was just gaining recognition in the sixteenth century,[5] seems a great deal more probable than this, although it is just as likely that Palladio simply took the ratio from Vitruvius,[6] without feeling any need to justify its use.

In one sense the golden section is easy to find in Renaissance work. It is highly probable that Serlio, in his drawing of a pentagonal church plan,[7] or Vignola, in his design for the Palazzo Farnese at Caprarola, used Euclid's construction for a pentagon, and this depends on making a golden section.[8] But pentagons are in fact rare in Renaissance architecture,[9] and even if they had been common, the use of the golden section in drawing them implies no understanding of it as an instrument of proportion rather than as a geometrical construction.

Osborne believes that 'the complicated mathematical properties of this

---

[1] But note Macody Lund's use of this principle in his theoretical reconstruction of Greek methods of design in *Ad Quadratum* (1921).

[2] E.g. in the cathedral at Ely, S. Lorenzo at Turin, and the mosque at Cordova.

[3] There are many examples in Dr Richter's *Literary Works of Leonardo da Vinci* (1939), vol. II. See Plate 7.

[4] *The Geometry of Art and Life* (1946), p. 59.

[5] *Architectural Principles in the Age of Humanism* (2nd ed.), pp. 115–16.

[6] *De architectura*, VI, iii, 3.   [7] *Libro primo d'architettura*, 1560–2.

[8] 'Elements', IV, 10–11.

[9] Wotton condemns pentagons except in military architecture, and says of Vignola's use of the pentagon that, 'as designs of such nature do more aim at rarity than commodity, so for my part I had rather admire than commend them' (*Elements of Architecture*, facsimile edition of 1903, p. 15).

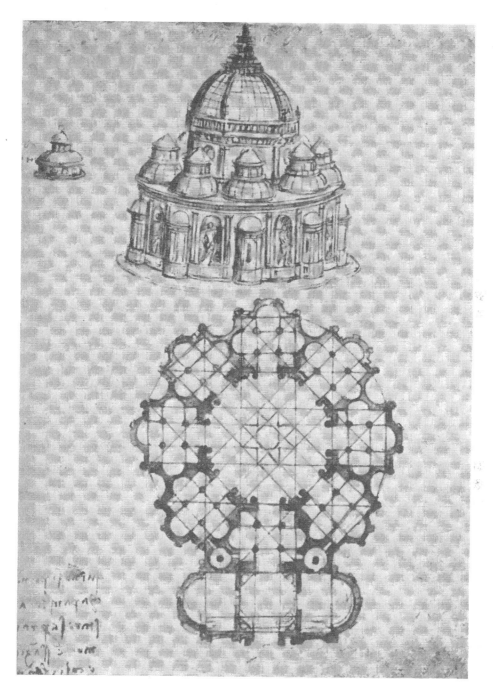

7. CHURCH PLAN BY LEONARDO DA VINCI

Proportions based on the θ series. (From the original in the Bibliothèque Nationale, Paris.)

proportion, the elaborate geometrical developments to which it leads, and its connexion with the "Fibonacci series", all contributed to give it a peculiar glamour and mystery which fascinated a mentality but newly emerging from the trammels of alchemy, hermetics, astrology, and mystic numbers'.[1]

Now there was, no doubt, plenty of mathematical interest in the golden section. The sixteenth-century French mathematician Finaeus falsely believed that it had given him the solution to several mathematical problems of the same character as squaring the circle.[2] Piero della Francesca, Pacioli, and later Kepler, in their studies of the five regular solids, learnt all that Euclid and Hypsicles had to teach them about the golden section.[3] Kepler described it in a much-quoted phrase as 'a precious gem, one of the two treasures of geometry'. Pacioli is said to have given it the name 'divina proportione', which Leonardo seems to have used in a more general sense.

But it is important to notice that although Pacioli's work on the regular solids, borrowed from Piero, was incorporated with his work on architecture in one volume which took the title *Divina proportione*, his discussion of the proportions of architecture and of the human figure appears to have been perfectly conventional, and based, not on the golden section, but on the ideas of Vitruvius.[4]

However interested some writers may have been in the golden section as mathematicians, there is little evidence that its value was appreciated in design, except as a purely mechanical means of constructing a regular pentagon. It is hardly an exaggeration to say that the golden section remained preserved like a fly in amber in very much the same mathematical context which Euclid had given it. It was not in the Renaissance, but in the nineteenth century, that the first real rediscovery of its uses outside this context seems to have been made.

---

[1] H. Osborne, *Theory of Beauty* (1952), p. 174.

[2] Cantor, *Vorlesungen über Geschichte der Mathematik* (2nd ed. 1900), vol. II, p. 377.

[3] In the thirteenth book of Euclid's 'Elements', and in the so-called 'fourteenth' book, nowadays attributed to Hypsicles.

[4] An account of Pacioli's work is given by Cantor (*Vorlesungen über Geschichte der Mathematik*, vol. II, pp. 341–4); and Professor Ghyka gives some quotations from Pacioli in 'Gothic canons of architecture', an article in the *Burlington Magazine*, March 1945.

CHAPTER IV

THE THEORY OF PROPORTION IN THE RENAISSANCE (2)

THE 'MUSICAL' ANALOGY

(A) ALBERTI

We now come to what is perhaps the most interesting aspect of Renaissance proportional theory, the 'musical' theory, with which Professor Wittkower has dealt at length.[1] We cannot use Professor Wittkower's term 'harmonic proportion' here, as this would lead to confusion with the mathematical sense in which the word 'harmonic' has already been used.

Alberti introduces his study of the subject in the following words:

'By the finishing I understand a certain mutual correspondence of those several lines by which the proportions are measured, whereof one is the length, the other the breadth and the other the height.

'The rule of these proportions is best gathered from those things in which we find Nature herself to be most compleat and admirable; and indeed I am every day more and more convinced of the truth of Pythagoras's saying, that Nature is sure to act consistently and with a constant analogy in all her operations: from whence I conclude the same numbers, by means of which the agreement of sounds affects our ears with delight, are the very same which please our eyes and our mind. We shall therefore borrow all our rules for the finishing of our proportions from the musicians, who are the greatest masters of this sort of numbers, and from those particular things wherein Nature shows herself most excellent and compleat: not that I shall look any further into these matters than is necessary for the purpose of the architect. . . .'[2]

An important point to notice here is that Alberti confines the use of 'musical' proportions, in theory at least, solely to the relationships between the three separate dimensions height, length and breadth.[3] He thus avoids completely any need to add or subtract the dimensions he is discussing, a requirement in which the theory of

[1] *Architectural Principles in the Age of Humanism*, part IV.

[2] *Ten Books on Architecture*, pp. 196–7.

[3] But not necessarily in practice. See Professor Wittkower's analysis of the façade of S. Maria Novella (*Architectural Principles in the Age of Humanism*, 2nd ed. p. 40).

proportion in architecture normally differs so completely from the theory of musical harmony.

Professor Wittkower, it is true, seems to treat Alberti's manipulation of ratios as applying to the subdivision of a single line, and speaks of the splitting up of proportions being for Alberti a 'spatial experience'.[1] But while this is a very natural development of Alberti's theory, it does not seem to be one which he makes himself.

Alberti later proceeds to give a list of the ratios permissible between the lengths and sides of rooms.[2] These consist of the ratios 1:1, 2:3 and 3:4 for short rooms, 2:1, 4:9 and 9:16 for medium rooms, and 3:1, 3:8 and 4:1 for long rooms. The following table gives the musical intervals to which these ratios correspond, together with some of their ancient Latin names which came down through Boethius and which are common in the Renaissance literature of the subject:

RATIO	LATIN NAME	MUSICAL INTERVAL
1:1		Unison
4:3	Sesquitertius	Fourth (diatessaron)
3:2	Sesquialter	Fifth (diapente)
16:9		
2:1	Duplus	Octave (diapason)
9:4		
8:3		Eleventh (diapason cum diatessaron)
3:1	Triplus	Twelfth (diapason cum diapente)
4:1	Quadruplus	Fifteenth (bisdiapason)

All of the ratios correspond to musical consonances except two, 16:9 and 9:4, which are equal respectively to $(4:3)^2$ and $(3:2)^2$. In Alberti's own words, the ratios 'are either innate with harmony itself, or produced from other proportions in a certain and regular manner.'[3]

An architect keeping to this list of ratios would ensure that the floors and ceilings of his rooms belonged to a limited number of distinct shapes. The next step was to determine the shape of the walls by fixing the height of the rooms. The problem here is to find three numbers, of which the ratio of any pair belongs to the list of prescribed ratios. This Alberti does by the method which Professor Wittkower describes as the 'generation of ratios', which goes back through Boethius to Nicomachus, and

[1] *Architectural Principles in the Age of Humanism*, 2nd ed. pp. 101–2.

[2] *Ten Books on Architecture*, pp. 197–8.

[3] The dissonance of 16:9 and 9:4 is stressed by Professor Wittkower as proof that Alberti did not try to translate music into architecture too literally (*Architectural Principles in the Age of Humanism*, 2nd ed. p. 102).

which seems so clumsy to modern eyes.[1] He works out for us a series of examples of groups of numbers related in this fashion:

$$
\begin{array}{ccc}
2 & 3 & 4 \\
3 & 4 & 6 \\
2 & 4 & 6 \\
2 & 3 & 6 \\
2 & 4 & 8 \\
\end{array}
$$

$$
\begin{array}{cccc}
2 & 3 & 4 & 8 \\
3 & 6 & 9 & 12 \\
\end{array}
$$

The ratio of any pair of numbers taken from any of these groups always belongs to the list of ratios.

Usually the smallest of three numbers represents the width of a room, the largest the length, and the intermediate number the height, although later on we are told that 'sometimes for the convenience of structures they are interchanged'.

Some surprise has been caused by the fact that as well as groups of three numbers Alberti also gives us groups of four numbers, and it has even been suggested that he is wandering off here into four-dimensional architecture.[2] A more commonplace but more probable explanation is that he is simply giving alternatives for the height of the room. Of the choice between 2, 4, 6 and 2, 3, 6, he says that architects select whichever 'is most agreeable to the circumstances of their structure'. The same is true of the choice between 3, 6, 12 and 3, 9, 12, which, now that the reader has had a chance to understand what he is doing, he combines as 3, 6, 9, 12.

What Alberti has really given us here is a series of scales. If we rewrite the groups of numbers thus

$$
\begin{array}{ccccccc}
2 \ 4 & 4 & 2 \ 4 & 2 & 2 \ 4 \ 8 & 2 \ 4 \ 8 & 3 \ 6 \ 12 \\
3 & 3 \ 6 & 6 & 3 \ 6 & & 3 & 9 \\
\end{array}
$$

it is quite clear that they are simply fragments of the double geometric progression

$$
\begin{array}{cccccccc}
1 & 2 & 4 & 8 & 16 & 32 & \cdots \\
 & 3 & 6 & 12 & 24 & \cdots \\
 & & 9 & 18 & 36 & \cdots \\
 & & & 27 & \cdots \\
\end{array}
$$

[1] For instance, Butler, in his review of Professor Wittkower's book (*R.I.B.A. Journal*, December 1951), found the 'generation of ratios' 'almost a bore'.

[2] 'Il envisage cependant des suites de quatre nombres, qui, si elles restent traduisibles en une suite de quatre notes, deviennent en revanche inapplicables à l'architecture, ou ne s'appliqueraient qu'à une architecture non-euclidienne, une architecture à quatre dimensions' (Michel, *La Pensée de L. B. Alberti*, Paris, 1930, pp. 454–5).

This progression is already familiar to us, and we have come across various ways of generating it.

Professor Wittkower shows how Francesco Giorgi obtained it, using an extraordinarily clumsy method borrowed from Plato's *Timaeus*.[1] In his myth describing the creation of the 'World Soul', Plato had explained how its structure had been determined mathematically by filling in harmonic and arithmetic means between successive terms of the two series of numbers 1, 2, 4, 8 and 1, 3, 9, 27.[2]

Giorgi, starting with 6, 12, 24, 48 and 6, 18, 54, 162, in order to avoid fractions, arrived at the series of numbers 6, 8, 9, 12, 16, 18, 24, 27, 32, 36, 48, 54, 81, 108, 162.[3] These numbers can be arranged in the pattern

$$
\begin{array}{ccccccc}
 & 8 & & 16 & & 32 & \\
6 & & 12 & & 24 & & 48 \\
 & 9 & & 18 & & 36 & \\
 & & & 27 & & 54 & & 108 \\
 & & & & & 81 & & & 162 \\
\end{array}
$$

and form part of the double geometric progression

$$
\begin{array}{ccccccc}
1 & & 2 & & 4 & & 8 & & 16 & & \cdots \\
 & & & 3 & & 6 & & 12 & & \cdots \\
 & & & & & 9 & & 18 & & \cdots \\
\end{array}
$$

which Alberti arrived at in a piecemeal fashion by the repetition of the ratios of musical consonances.

The reader will find that if he looks at this pattern of numbers as a sort of chessboard, then Alberti's prescribed ratios correspond to certain definite chess-moves. Thus the ratio 2:1 corresponds to one horizontal step, the ratio 3:2 corresponds to one diagonal step downwards and to the right, the ratio 9:4 corresponds to two steps in the same direction, and so on. The art of generating ratios becomes the art of combining two or more chess-moves to make one.

---

[1] *Architectural Principles in the Age of Humanism*, 2nd ed. pp. 91–2 and 98–9.

[2] The interpolation of harmonic and arithmetic means between successive pairs of terms of a single geometric progression automatically extends the progression two steps into a second dimension, e.g.

$$
\begin{array}{cccc}
\dfrac{\phi^2}{2} & \dfrac{\phi^3}{2} & \dfrac{\phi^4}{2} & \cdots \\[2mm]
1 \quad\quad \phi & \phi^2 & \cdots \\[2mm]
\dfrac{2}{\phi} & 2 & 2\phi & \cdots \\
\end{array}
$$

[3] *Architectural Principles in the Age of Humanism*; plate 36b gives a diagram from Giorgi's *De Harmonia Mundi* (1525).

He will also see that if he restricts himself to chess-moves consisting of not more than two steps taken horizontally or diagonally, he has in fact restricted himself to Alberti's list of prescribed ratios, with the addition of 9:8, the 'tone'.[1]

Looking at the matter from a slightly different point of view, if we isolate any group of numbers like

```
        8       16                                    .      .
  6        12        24      forming the pattern       .      .      .
     9        18                                          .      .
```

on the chess-board, we will find that the ratio between any pair of them belongs to the prescribed list, with the addition of 9:8. We can therefore treat this group as a sort of sub-scale, from which we can select any three convenient numbers to represent the breadth, height and length of a room.

In one passage Alberti explains that his ratios should be used, 'not confusedly and indistinctly, but in such manner as to be constantly and every way agreeable to harmony: as, for instance, in the elevation of a room which is twice as long as broad, they [architects] make use, not of those numbers which compose the triple, but of those only which form the duple...'.[2] Now, it is quite clear that the number 16 'composes the duple' 9:18, in the sense that the numbers 9, 16, 18 all belong to the same sub-scale. It is equally clear that it does not 'compose the triple' 9:27, since 16 and 27 are too far apart on the chess-board to belong to the same sub-scale.[3]

The picture of the chess-board is useful for explaining and extending Alberti's theoretical treatment of ratios. In practice it would be a simple matter to translate the chess-moves into operations with an actual scale of dimensions. Whether it would be worth while doing so is another matter, as the geometrical progression concerned is not well enough equipped with additive properties to form a really flexible system of proportion. This fact explains why Alberti did not rely wholly on the 'musical' theory of proportion, and underlies the eventual failure of the theory.

Before we leave Alberti's theory of proportion, something must be said about the use of 'means', the rules of which 'are derived not from harmony or the natural proportions of bodies, but are borrowed elsewhere for determining the three relations of an apartment'. The means to which Alberti attaches most importance are the arithmetic, geometric and harmonic means.

[1] This is the only ratio which Alberti gives in his list of 'musical' ratios (IX, v) but excludes from his list of 'architectural' ratios (IX, vi). It appears, however, in his account of the generation of the ratios 4:9 (4:8:9) and 9:16 (9:18:16).

[2] *Ten Books on Architecture*, p. 199.

[3] From this point of view all the numbers which 'compose the triple' also 'compose the duple', but not all of those which 'compose the duple' also 'compose the triple'.

Now while the 'musical' system of proportion and a system based on the use of means are not identical, they do overlap to some extent. Thus Alberti's own examples of means are based on numbers which are consistent with his own 'musical' system. He gives the arithmetic progression 4, 6, 8, the geometric progression 4, 6, 9, and the harmonic progression 30, 40, 60 or 3, 4, 6. Furthermore, in all the examples of groups of three numbers with which he illustrates the 'musical' system, the intermediate number is in every case a 'mean' of the other two. Thus 3 is the arithmetic mean of 2 and 4, and the harmonic mean of 2 and 6; 4 is the harmonic mean of 3 and 6, the arithmetic mean of 2 and 6, and the geometric mean of 2 and 8.

To go back to our chess-board, 12 is the geometric mean of 6 and 24, 8 and 18, and also 9 and 16. Not all the groups of numbers which can be obtained are related in this way, but enough to show that the system of means, used in conjunction with a system of prescribed ratios, was not a bad substitute for Alberti's method of generating ratios, and very much simpler for the practical architect. This is the reason why the 'generation of ratios' disappears from the literature of architectural theory after Alberti, though we continue to hear quite a lot about the 'means'.

(B) PALLADIO

Palladio's work requires less detailed consideration here than that of Alberti. Coming a century later, when the first impetus of the Renaissance had been expended, Palladio's theoretical contribution seems comparatively cautious.

The counter-reformation stressed the importance of authority, and in architecture this meant the written word of Vitruvius and the physical remains of antiquity. So we find Palladio keeping within safe limits in his book, and avoiding the aesthetic speculation which delighted Alberti. Where he does depart from Vitruvius, he relies on the measurement of classical buildings.[1] His list of ratios recommended for the shapes of rooms owes more to Vitruvius than it does to Alberti.[2] He completely avoids considering the 'musical' theory and Alberti's other ideas on proportion, except for the use of the 'means', arithmetic, geometric or harmonic, with which he determines the heights of vaulted rooms.[3]

As we have seen, in conjunction with Alberti's prescribed ratios for the shapes of rooms, this use of the means did constitute a rough and ready system of proportion.

[1] E.g. 'The measures and proportions of each of these orders I shall separately set down; not so much according to Vitruvius, as to the observations I have made on several ancient edifices' (*The Four Books of Architecture*, transl. by Ware, I, xii, p. 11).   [2] The circle, the square, $\sqrt{2}$, $\frac{4}{3}$, $\frac{3}{2}$, $\frac{5}{3}$, 2 (I, xxi, p. 27).

[3] 'We'll however make use of each of these heights, according as they may suit with convenience, that several rooms of different dimensions may be so made as to have all their vaults of an equal height, and the said vaults to be nevertheless proportionable to them; from which will result both beauty to the eye, and convenience for the floors that are placed thereon, since they'll be all level' (I, xxiii, p. 29, Ware's translation).

Unlike Alberti, Palladio restricted the means to the heights of rooms only, thus ensuring that all vaulted rooms were higher than they were broad; and he insisted that rooms with flat ceilings should be as high as they were broad: these facts may have hindered the spread of his ideas in colder countries.[1]

In spite of this cautious attitude, the following passage shows his debt to Alberti: 'Beauty will result from the form and correspondence of the whole with respect to the several parts, of the parts with regard to each other, and of these again to the whole; that the structure may appear an entire and compleat body, wherein each member agrees with the other....'[2]

This idea was taken a step further by Palladio himself, who applied it to the internal planning of houses: 'But the large rooms with the middling, and those with the small ought to be so distributed that, as I have elsewhere said, one part of the fabric may correspond with the other, and that so the body of the edifice may have in itself a certain convenience in its members, that may render the whole beautiful and graceful.'[3] Taken by itself this passage is so vague as to be almost meaningless, but studied in connexion with Palladio's own practice, which we are now to consider, it seems to refer to what Professor Wittkower calls Palladio's 'fugal' system of proportion.[4]

However cautious Palladio was in theory, in practice he seems to have experimented freely in 'musical' proportion. This fact appears to have been rediscovered by O. B. Scamozzi in the eighteenth century, in the course of writing his book, *Le fabbriche e i disegni di Andrea Palladio*. The first volume is concerned with buildings in the town of Vicenza, on restricted sites where there was little freedom to experiment. The second and third volumes deal with Palladio's country houses, and in the preface to the third volume an account of Alberti's 'musical' theory is given, with the suggestion that Palladio used Alberti's rules in proportioning his buildings.[5]

After this, references to the ratios of the musical consonances become frequent in Scamozzi's text, not only in connexion with the plans, where they are often supported by the dimensions of rooms given by Palladio himself, but also in connexion with the elevations, where Scamozzi had to rely on his own measurements of the buildings. Incidentally, the danger of having to rely on measurements in studying the

---

[1] Wotton, often critical of Italian domestic planning, remarks: '...though the least error or offence that can be committed against sight is an excess of height, yet that fault is nowhere of small importance, because it is the greatest offence against the purse' (*Elements of Architecture*, facsimile edition of 1903, p. 95).

[2] *The Four Books of Architecture*, I, i, p. 1.   [3] *Ibid*. II, ii, p. 38.

[4] *Architectural Principles in the Age of Humanism*, 2nd ed. pp. 110ff.

[5] 'Forse il Palladio, studiosissimo, com'è stato, di quell'Autore, avrà adoperate le regole da esso Alberti, e da altri Autori indicate nel proporzionare il tutto insieme de' suoi Edifizj, e nel combinare con armoniche misure tutte le parti che li compongono' (*Le fabbriche e i disegni di Andrea Palladio*, vol. III, p. 4).

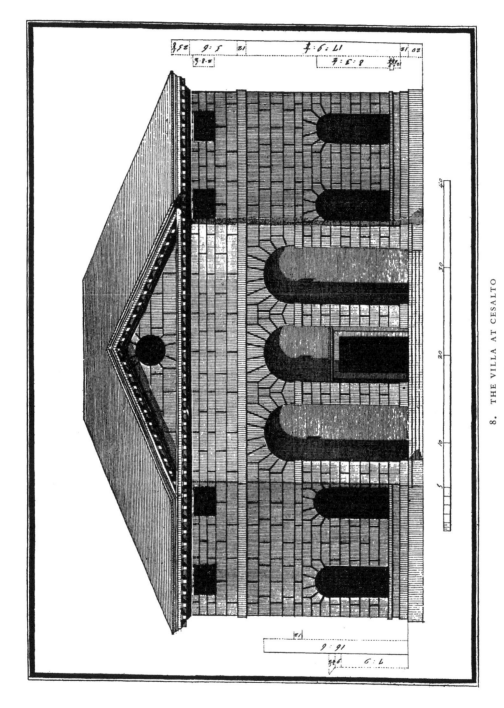

8. THE VILLA AT CESALTO

A square superimposed on a double square. (From O. B. Scamozzi's *Le fabbriche e i disegni di Andrea Palladio*, pl. xxvii, vol. iii.)

62

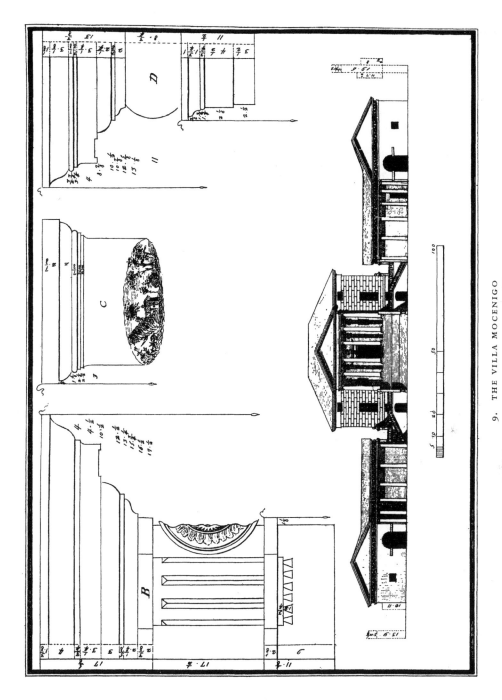

9. THE VILLA MOCENIGO

A square superimposed on a double square. (From O. B. Scamozzi's *Le fabbriche e i disegni di Andrea Palladio*, pl. xlii, vol. iii.)

63

intended proportions of buildings is well illustrated by Scamozzi, who gives frequent tables comparing the dimensions given in Palladio's drawings and those of the buildings as they were executed. Very often the intended dimensions agree with the 'musical' theory of proportion, while those of the buildings themselves do not.

Scamozzi often traces ratios like 2 : 1 and 3 : 2 in Palladio's elevations. An arrangement which appears several times consists in placing a square in the centre of a double square, leaving two smaller double squares forming wings on either side. This seems to occur, for instance, in the main elevations of the Villa Mocenigo and the Villa at Cesalto.[1]

Scamozzi was, however, on firmer ground in discussing the proportions of rooms in Palladio's designs, and to these Professor Wittkower gives a great deal of attention. Where Palladio gives us the dimensions of the rooms in his designs, we very often find that not only do the ratios of the length and breadth of individual rooms conform to the 'musical' theory of proportion, but the majority of the dimensions in a plan belong to a geometric progression. Of this fact Professor Wittkower remarks that 'the systematic linking of one room to the other by harmonic proportions was the fundamental novelty of Palladio's architecture....Those proportional relationships which other architects had harnessed for the two dimensions of a façade or the three dimensions of a single room were employed by him to integrate a whole structure.'[2]

We may perhaps add, however, that Palladio omits the overall dimensions from his plans, and so avoids the problem of adding the separate dimensions together just as effectively as Alberti. His system of proportion integrates the whole structure in the sense that it links the parts, or separate rooms, to each other, but it still fails to relate them to the whole.

Here are some examples of groups of dimensions which appear in Palladio's plans:

Villa Godi[3]	16				
		24			
			36		
Villa Malcontenta[4]		16		32	
	12		24		

---

[1] Of the Villa at Cesalto, Scamozzi says in a footnote: 'La proporzione, che rilevasi nel presente Prospetto fra la lunghezza e l'altezza, è quasi quella che si ravvisa fra l'uno e il due, cioè la ottava; e la medesima proporzione troviamo fra la larghezza della Loggia, e ognuna delle due Ale' (vol. III, p. 39). The elevation of the Villa Mocenigo is subdivided still further, and the ratio 2 : 3, or the fifth, is referred to as well as the octave (vol. III, p. 52). See Plates 8 and 9.

[2] *Architectural Principles in the Age of Humanism*, 2nd ed. p. 113.

[3] Wittkower, p. 112; O. B. Scamozzi, vol. II, p. 27.

[4] Wittkower, p. 113; O. B. Scamozzi, vol. III, p. 8.

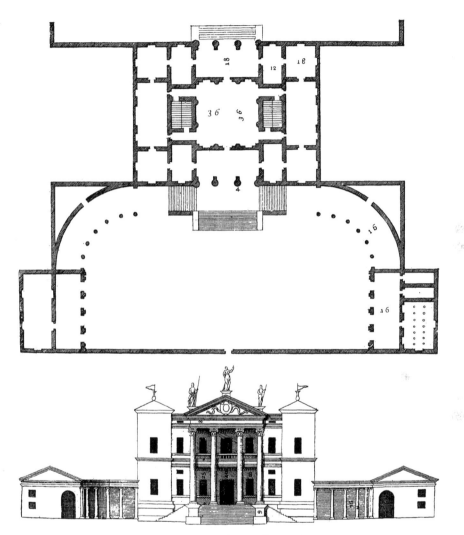

10. THE VILLA TIENE AT CIGOGNA

(From Palladio's *I quattro libri dell'architettura*, translated by Isaac Ware, 1738; pl. xlv.)

5

65

S A

Villa Emo[1]   16

                    12   24   48

Villa Tiene[2]   16

                    12

                            18   36

Villa Pisani[3]   16   32

                    24

            18

These are obviously fragments of the familiar double geometric progression which we have already encountered in the work of Alberti. Sometimes a triple geometric progression is found:

Villa Sarego[4]   4   8   16

                            12   24

                        9   18

                                    27

                    10   20   40

                        15

(c) LATER HISTORY OF THE MUSICAL ANALOGY

Other sixteenth-century advocates of simply commensurable proportions were Francesco Giorgi, Vignola, and Jerome Cardan, the mathematician and philosopher. Of these, Giorgi, in his *Memorandum for S. Francesco della Vigna*, in which the 1, 3, 9, 27 progression plays a prominent part, used the names of musical intervals to describe the ratios whose use he recommended;[5] while Vignola persuaded himself that the most graceful examples of the orders surviving from antiquity were those with the simplest commensurable proportions.[6]

---

[1] Wittkower, p. 114; O. B. Scamozzi, vol. III, p. 24.

[2] Wittkower, p. 114; O. B. Scamozzi, vol. III, p. 21. See Plate 10.

[3] Wittkower, p. 117; O. B. Scamozzi, vol. II, p. 14.

[4] Wittkower, p. 117; O. B. Scamozzi, vol. III, p. 13. See Plate 11.

[5] E.g. 'The length of the nave, which will be 27, will have a triple proportion which makes a diapason and a diapente.' 'Turning now to the height, I commend...60 feet or 12 paces, in the sesquitertial proportion to the width, which results in a diatessaron, a celebrated and melodious harmony.' The memorandum is translated in full in *Architectural Principles in the Age of Humanism*, 2nd ed., appendix I, pp. 136–8.

[6] '...Questi tutti insieme considerandoli, e con diligenti misure esaminandoli, ho trovato quelli, che al giudizio comune appajono più belli, e con più grazia si appresentano agl'occhi nostri; questi ancora avere certa corrispondenza, e proporzione di numeri insieme meno intrigata, anzi ciascun minimo membro, misurare li maggiori in tante lor parti appunto....' This passage from the preface to Vignola's *Regole dei*

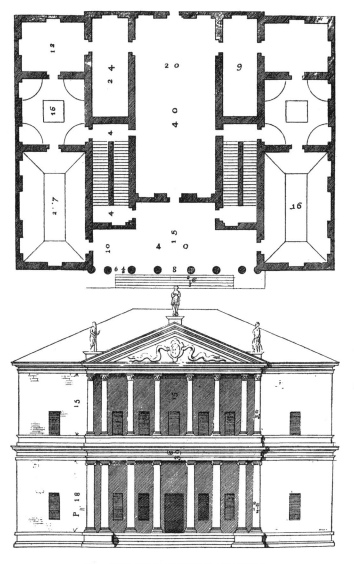

11. THE VILLA SAREGO AT MIEGA

(From Palladio's *I quattro libri dell'architettura*, translated by Isaac Ware, 1738; pl. l.)

Cardan's work is of particular interest, as he attempted to give a theoretical explanation of the value of simple ratios in both musical harmony and architectural proportion. Cardan's theory, of which echoes are still sometimes heard today, was that simply commensurable proportions, whether they entered the mind through the ears or the eyes, were pleasing because they were intelligible.[1] This elegant theory will have to be discussed later on in some detail. Although later discoveries have shown it to be entirely false, it gives an explanation of the unquestioned facts of musical consonance, as well as of the supposed facts of architectural proportion, thus encouraging unqualified belief in the latter. The acceptance of the theory was all the more natural because the use of simple ratios in architecture actually has something to be said for it, though we now know that the reasons for this are entirely different from the reasons for using simple ratios in musical harmony.

The classical theory of proportion in Italy was eclipsed during the height of the Baroque period, but traces of it seem to have survived in the teaching of the Treviso school.[2] The use of the means, and particularly the harmonic mean, survived for determining the heights of rooms.[3] A revival of the theory of simply commensurable proportions occurred in the latter part of the eighteenth century, stimulated partly by French influence.

The theory had been carried outside Italy as part of the main body of architectural theory, but it took comparatively little root. By the time the real flow of archi-

cinque ordini d'architettura is quoted by Gwilt in the 1862 edition of Chambers's Treatise on Civil Architecture, p. 138n. It can be translated roughly: 'Considering them all together, and measuring them carefully, I have discovered that those which are usually considered most beautiful and most graceful to our eyes, are the ones having a definite relationship and the least intricate numerical proportions; in other words, where the smallest parts measure the larger parts exactly.'

[1] 'Cognita in auditu vocantur consonantia, in visu pulchra. Quid igitur est pulchritudo? Res visui perfecte cognita, incognita enim amare non possumus: ea autem agnoscit visus quae simplici constant proportione dupla, tripla, quadrupla, sesquialtera, sesquitertia, ut de humana facie diximus: cum igitur columnis ea ratione dispositis, aut arboribus, aut faciei partibus, illico in illis aequalitatem et symmetriam intelligit delectatur. Est enim delectatio in cognoscendo, ut non cognoscendo tristitia. Porro obscura imperfectaque ob id non cognoscuntur, quod sint infinita, confusa, indeterminataque: talia igitur cum sint infinita, cognosci nequeunt, igitur imperfecta non possunt delectare, nec esse pulchra. Pulchrum igitur quicquid commensuratum est, delectare etiam solet' (De subtilitate, 1559, book XIII, p. 494). Translated fairly literally this becomes: 'In hearing the known is called consonance, in seeing beauty. What therefore is beauty? The thing perfectly known by sight, for we cannot love the unknown. Now the sight recognizes what is related by the simple ratios 2:1, 3:1, 4:1, 3:2, 4:3, as we have said in speaking of the human face. It is therefore delighted to observe equality and symmetry in the method of arranging columns or trees or the parts of the face. For there is delight in knowing, as there is sadness in not knowing. Moreover, the obscure and imperfect are not understood, because they are undefined, confused and indeterminate. When they are undefined they cannot be understood, so the imperfect cannot give delight, or be beautiful. The beautiful is therefore something whose dimensions are commensurable, and it gives delight.'   [2] See Architectural Principles in the Age of Humanism, 2nd ed. p. 128.

[3] The use of means alone, without any system of prescribed ratios, is merely a useless vestige of Alberti's generation of ratios.

12. CORINTHIAN ORDER FROM BARCA'S 'PROPORZIONE IN ARCHITETTURA'

Repetition of ratios; the subdivision 3 : 2 : 2 is repeated five times.

69

tectural theory from Italy to other countries had begun, original work on the theory of proportion was largely at an end, and the influence of Vitruvius was already dominant.

The musical analogy is, however, represented in France by the work of François Blondel in the seventeenth century.[1] Then a revival of interest occurred in the eighteenth century, associated with neo-classicism, and is shown in the work of Briseux[2] and Laugier.[3] This revival spread back to Italy, where, as we have seen, O. B. Scamozzi rediscovered Palladio's use of a musical system of proportion. The work of Barca also[4] is of considerable value, however little interest it may have aroused at the time. Although Barca's theory of commensurability is not very different from Cardan's, to some extent he provided an answer to the eighteenth-century critics, and anticipated a modern theory of proportion, so his work will be considered in more detail below.

In England the picture is slightly different. The high Renaissance arrived so late that it formed a sort of premature neo-classicism. In the same way the musical theory of proportion survived into the eighteenth century without requiring a revival. It was then destroyed, along with the general theory of proportion of which it formed a part, at just the time when this revival was taking place in France and Italy.

The musical analogy was perhaps introduced into England by Haydock, in his translation of Lomazzo's work.[5] Hogarth included Lomazzo among the writers on human proportion who 'have not only puzzled mankind with a heap of minute unnecessary divisions, but also with a strange *notion* that those divisions are govern'd by the laws of music...'.[6] Sir Henry Wotton spoke of 'eurythmia' as 'that agreeable harmony between the breadth, length, and height of all the rooms of the fabric, which suddenly, where it is, taketh every beholder by the secret power of proportion'.[7] He lets us into the secret in speaking of doors and windows:

'These inlets of men and of light I couple together, because I find their due dimensions brought under one rule by Leone Alberti, a learned searcher, who from the School of Pythagoras (where it was a fundamental maxim that the images of all things are latent in numbers) doth determine the comeliest proportion between breadths and heights; reducing symmetry to symphony, and the harmony of sound to a kind of harmony in sight after this manner: The two principal consonances that most ravish the ear are by the consent of all nature the fifth and the octave. Whereof the first riseth radically from the proportion between two and three. The other from

---

[1] *Cours d'architecture* (Paris, 1675–83).   [2] *Traité du Beau essentiel dans les arts* (1752).

[3] *Observations sur l'architecture* (La Haye, 1765).

[4] *Proporzione in architettura* (1806).

[5] Richard Haydock, *A Tracte containing the Artes of curious Paintinge, Carving, and Building* (1598).

[6] William Hogarth, *The Analysis of Beauty* (1753), p. 91 in the edition of 1955.

[7] Sir Henry Wotton, *Elements of Architecture*, facsimile edition of 1903, p. 95.

the double interval between one and two, or between two and four, etc. Now if we shall transport these proportions from audible to visible objects, and apply them as they fall fittest (the nature of the place considered) namely in some windows and doors, the symmetry of two to three in their breadth and length, in others, the double as aforesaid, there will indubitably result from either a graceful and harmonious contentment to the eye.'[1]

The fact that Inigo Jones followed Palladio in putting the musical analogy into practice is shown by such examples as the double cube of the Banqueting House at Whitehall, the simple proportions of the rooms of the Queen's House at Greenwich,[2] and the double cube room at Wilton House, which was completed from Inigo Jones's design by Webb.[3]

The survival of the musical analogy into the eighteenth century in England is shown in the work of Robert Morris.[4] While Palladio had only gone as far as prescribing certain ratios for the plans of rooms, Morris laid down 'seven definite forms of parallelepipeds proper for building'.[5] These had their sides in the ratios:

$$1:1:1 \text{ (cube)}, \quad 2:2:3, \quad 1:1:2 \text{ (double cube)}, \quad 1:2:3, \quad 2:3:4, \quad 3:4:5 \text{ and } 3:4:6.$$

The difficulty of the heights of rooms in the English climate was overcome by allowing these parallelepipeds to be placed any way up.

The type of empiricism found in the work of Sir William Chambers, however, is far more usual in the eighteenth century in England. Not only the musical analogy and the use of simply commensurable ratios were discarded in this period, but also the general theory of proportion as a cause of 'natural beauty', and finally the Renaissance theory of objective beauty itself were overthrown. This process was spread over a long period. The musical analogy, as the weakest link in the chain, was the first to go, but the final collapse of the Renaissance theory of architecture and Renaissance aesthetics was complete in the nineteenth century.

Before this collapse of the theory of proportion is discussed, it is worth pointing out that some interest in the use of simply commensurable ratios did in fact survive it, as we shall see when we come to consider the ideas of some nineteenth-century writers on proportion. This may well suggest that in practice there is something to be said for the use of these ratios, even though the theory which was intended to explain this turned out to be inadequate.

[1] Sir Henry Wotton, *Elements of Architecture*, facsimile edition of 1903, pp. 42–3. An extraordinary injustice has been done to Sir Henry Wotton by the suggestion that his work on architecture is a mere paraphrase of Vitruvius.   [2] Margaret Whinney, *Renaissance Architecture in England* (1952), p. 29.

[3] Christopher Hussey, *English Country Houses* (1951), p. 97.

[4] Robert Morris, *Lectures on Architecture* (1734–6).

[5] Edward L. Garbett, *Principles of Design in Architecture* (1850), p. 39 in the 9th edition of 1906.

CRITICISMS OF RENAISSANCE THEORY

(A) THE MUSICAL ANALOGY

The musical analogy starts from the fact that groups of notes in music produced, for instance, by strings whose lengths are simply commensurable please the ears. It assumes that this fact of consonance has a psychological cause, and that the mind itself recognizes simple ratios and is pleased by them, whereas it finds more complicated mathematical ratios puzzling. If it is merely the abstract relationship of simple commensurability which pleases the mind, then there is no reason to suppose that the simple commensurability of visible dimensions in architecture will not please the mind through the eye just as effectively as musical consonance pleases it through the ear.

Such, roughly, is the theory of the musical analogy, namely, the transferring of proportions from the audible to the visible, introduced by Alberti and elaborated by Cardan. Exactly how literally this analogy is taken is not important to us at the moment. Barca, for instance, writing at the end of the eighteenth century, condemns the musical analogy in its most literal form, as expounded by Briseux.[1] While stressing the difference between music and architecture, he still insists on the use of simply commensurable ratios in both.

The attack on the theory of the musical analogy started seriously in the seventeenth century with Perrault, who opposed the views of François Blondel. Perrault discussed the problem of proportion at length in the preface to his book on the orders. He objected that the 'knowledge which we have, by means of the ear, of what results from the proportion of two strings, wherein the harmony consists, is quite different from the knowledge we have, by the eye, of what arises from the proportion of the parts of which a column is composed...'.[2] The ear is not in fact able to pass on to the mind any information about mathematical ratios at all.

On the other hand, certain proportions 'make the delicacy and agreement of sounds in music, which depend not upon us, but are such as nature has fixed and established with so precise an exactness, that they cannot be altered without immediate offence to the least curious ear'.[3] But in architecture, in the proportions of the orders for instance, 'the architect has a sufficient latitude to augment or diminish the dimensions of the parts, as occasion shall require'.[4] In short, in music simply

---

[1] A. Barca, *Proporzione in architettura*, pp. v–vi.

[2] Claude Perrault, *Ordonnance des cinq espèces de colonnes* (1683), translated by John James as *A Treatise of the Five Orders of Columns in Architecture* (1722), p. iv.

[3] *Ibid.* p. iii.

[4] *Ibid.* p. ii.

commensurable ratios please the mind without its being conscious of them as ratios at all. In architecture wide variations in ratio are tolerated without discomfort, although the mind can in this case form an estimate of the value of the ratios concerned. The cases are quite different, and no analogy is possible.

The attack was taken up again by several British critics in the middle of the eighteenth century. Hogarth, for instance, ridiculed the application of the musical analogy, or, indeed, any system of mathematical proportions, to the human figure.[1] Sir William Chambers added a new argument to those of Perrault. Unlike Perrault himself, Chambers used minutes to express the proportions of the details of the orders. In discussing his reasons for doing this, he explained that many people 'prefer the method of measuring by equal parts, imagining beauty to depend on the simplicity and accuracy of the relations existing between the whole body and its members, and alleging that dimensions which have evident affinities are better remembered than those whose relations are too complicated to be immediately apprehended. With regard to the former of these suppositions it is evidently false, for the real relations subsisting between dissimilar figures have no connection with the apparent ones.'[2] In other words, any abstract mathematical relationships which might exist between the dimensions of an object would be concealed from the eye by the effects of perspective.

Lord Kames went to some trouble to dispose of the musical analogy: '...we have no reason to presume, that there is any natural analogy between the proportions that please in a building and the proportions of strings that produce concordant sounds. Let us take, for example, an octave, produced by two similar strings, the one double of the other in length: this is the most perfect of all concords; and yet I know not that the proportion of one to two is agreeable in any two parts of a building.'[3]

After this point-blank denial that the most pleasing ratio of music produces any pleasure at all in architecture, Lord Kames makes Perrault's point about pleasing proportions in architecture not being precisely defined as those in music are. He adds that this is just as well for our comfort, since, owing to the effect of perspective, apparent proportions vary continuously as we move about: 'I need go no further for a proof than the very room I occupy at present; for every step I take varies to me, in appearance, the proportion of length to breadth; at that rate, I should not be happy but in one precise spot, where the proportion appears agreeable.'[4]

Later eighteenth-century writers, such as Alison,[5] were content to dismiss the

---

[1] William Hogarth, *Analysis of Beauty*, pp. 90–1 in the edition of 1955.
[2] Sir William Chambers, *Treatise on Civil Architecture* (1759); p. 123 in the edition of 1862.
[3] Henry Home, Lord Kames, *Elements of Criticism*, pp. 436–7 in the 11th edition of 1839.
[4] *Ibid.* p. 438.   [5] Archibald Alison, *On Taste* (1790).

musical analogy more lightly. But it was not until half-way through the nineteenth century that Garbett showed how the final answer to the theory of the musical analogy was to be given: 'Why should the height and breadth of a window have a certain simple ratio to each other? Because, says Vitruvius, two strings of the same thickness and tension, having their lengths in this same ratio, will yield concordant notes. The logic is truly admirable; but it was a very fair deduction for the science of that day, and only unfit for the present because we happen to know *why* the notes harmonise, and that it is for a reason which has nothing at all analogous to it in the case of the window...'.[1]

This was apparently written before Helmholtz had published his work on musical consonance. At any rate we now know that consonance can be explained simply as the absence of unpleasant beats between the partials of the notes which are reproduced by certain membranes of the ear itself.[2] It is thus primarily a physiological phenomenon depending on the structure of the ear, and not purely a psychological phenomenon depending on the recognition of simple ratios by the mind itself. There is therefore no reason at all for any analogy between proportion in architecture and harmony in music, and the suspicions of Perrault and others are completely confirmed.

What really requires explaining is why a belief in the musical analogy and in the efficacy of commensurable proportions continued so long, and, indeed, survives today. That commensurable proportions have a certain usefulness can be explained, but we have to accept the fact, suggested by Lord Kames and confirmed experimentally by Fechner, that such proportions are not pleasing to the eye in themselves; like the golden section, they are to be considered merely as a means to an end, a point of view which Barca seems to have anticipated, though he wrongly regarded simply commensurable proportions as the only means to that end.[3]

If we decide that the end of proportion is the repetition of shapes and ratios in order to create unity in a design, it becomes a comparatively elementary matter to explain the value of simple commensurability as a means to that end. In the simpler applications of the theory, the restriction of the designer to simply commensurable ratios both provides him with ratios which are easy to manipulate, and ensures their frequent repetition. In the more complicated applications like Alberti's generation of ratios and Palladio's 'fugal' system of proportion, the repetition of ratios is not left to chance, but is ensured by methods which give to the dimensions of the design the pattern of proportional relationships of a geometric progression.

[1] Edward L. Garbett, *Principles of Design in Architecture*, p. 38 in the 9th edition of 1906. The old error that Vitruvius was responsible for the musical analogy is repeated here.

[2] Helmholtz, *Sensations of Tone* (1862). A. Wood, *The Physical Basis of Music* (1913), ch. VII. Sir James Jeans, *Science and Music* (1937).

[3] A. Barca, *Proporzione in architettura.*

While this explains the partial success of the theory of simple commensurability, and accounts for our feeling that there must be something in it, it also explains why this success has been so very limited. This is evidently due to the mathematical fact that geometric progressions based on whole numbers are deficient in additive properties, so that systems of proportion derived from them are likely to lack flexibility. As we have seen, in the most consistent applications of the 'musical analogy', namely, those of Alberti and Palladio, the problem of adding smaller dimensions together to form larger ones is avoided. Alberti limits himself to considering the three separate dimensions of individual rooms. Although Palladio often deals with a succession of rooms in plan, we have no evidence as to how he dealt with the problem of adding their dimensions together to form the overall dimensions of the house of which they were parts.

This is the real reason why the Renaissance theory of commensurable proportions was not wholly successful. It was, however, a valuable experiment in the indirect approach to the problem of proportion through linear dimensions rather than geometrical shapes, and so it forms an introduction to the analytical methods of today.

Before leaving the Renaissance theory of proportion, we have to consider the decay of the general theory of which the musical analogy formed only a part.

(B) THE GENERAL THEORY OF PROPORTION

The musical analogy is only a part, and not a necessary part, of a wider theory of proportion. This theory rested on a foundation of certain aesthetic principles: beauty was believed to spring from real qualities of external objects, and proportion was believed to be one of these qualities; indeed, proportion and beauty were sometimes almost identified.

This is not the place for a detailed account of the slow attrition of the objective theory of beauty itself, of Hume's attempt to show how an objective theory of beauty could be retained in spite of varying standards of taste,[1] and of the final victory of complete subjectivism in Alison's theory of expression.[2] What is important to us is

---

[1] David Hume, *Four Dissertations* (1757). Hume's ideas have often been misunderstood. The following passage is sometimes quoted as a statement of his own view, but it is in fact a statement of the view he is about to oppose: 'Beauty is no quality in things themselves: it exists merely in the mind which contemplates them; and each mind perceives a different beauty.... To seek the real beauty, or real deformity, is as fruitless an enquiry as to pretend to ascertain the real sweet or the real bitter...' (pp. 208–9). Hume's own view is shown by the following passage: 'Though it be certain, that beauty and deformity, no more than sweet and bitter, are not qualities in objects, but belong entirely to the sentiment, internal or external; it must be allowed that there are certain qualities in objects, which are fitted by nature to produce those particular feelings...' (p. 217).
[2] Alison, *On Taste*.

the fact that from the seventeenth century onwards most writers felt that subjective elements play at least some part in controlling our sense of beauty. They found it convenient to adopt Plato's distinction between absolute and relative beauty.[1]

This distinction was given a classical statement by Sir Christopher Wren: 'There are two causes of beauty, natural and customary: natural is from geometry, consisting in uniformity (that is, equality) and proportion. Customary beauty is begotten by the use of our senses to those objects which are usually pleasing to us for other causes; as familiarity, or particular inclination, breeds a love to things not in themselves lovely.'[2]

Uniformity means here what we should probably call symmetry. But the point which concerns us here is that Wren placed proportion, as well, firmly among the causes of 'natural' beauty. His contemporary Perrault took the opposite view, anticipating the ruin of the Renaissance theory of proportion. Perrault agreed that symmetry was a cause of natural beauty; but he distinguished it carefully from proportion 'which is difficult to be perceived', and which 'consists in the relative conformity of the proportional parts, such as the dimensions of the parts in respect of each other, or of the whole'.[3] Unlike Wren, Perrault held that proportion in this sense was not a cause of natural beauty, and that its effects were solely due to custom.

Much of the discussion of proportion in the following century was concerned with deciding whether Wren or Perrault was right, and whether proportion was pleasing to the eye in itself, or indirectly through the operation of some other factor.

An important alternative to custom as a cause of the beauty of proportion was given by Bishop Berkeley, who put forward the theory that beautiful proportions are determined by fitness for purpose: 'And, in effect, have we not learned from this digression, that as there is no beauty without proportion, so proportions are to be esteemed just and true, only as they are relative to some certain use or end, their aptitude and subordination to which end is, at bottom, that which makes them please and charm?'[4] Berkeley thus anticipated the doctrine of functionalism in the early eighteenth century.

Meanwhile Hutcheson supported Wren's view of proportion: 'As to the works of art, were we to run through the various artificial contrivances or structures, we should constantly find the foundation of the beauty which appears in them, to be some kind of uniformity, or unity of proportion among the parts, and of each part

---

[1] *Philebus*, 51 B.

[2] This passage from Wren's first tract on architecture in the *Parentalia* was reprinted in James Elmes's *Memoirs of the Life and Works of Sir Christopher Wren* (1823), p. 119.

[3] Claude Perrault (transl. by James), *A Treatise of the Five Orders of Architecture*, p. vi.

[4] George Berkeley, *Alciphron, or the Minute Philosopher* (1732), vol. I, p. 182.

to the whole.'[1] He denied that the sense of beauty could be affected by custom, and rejected Berkeley's theory of fitness.

Lord Kames, while agreeing that fitness or utility was a source of 'relative' beauty, insisted that proportion, together with regularity, simplicity, uniformity and order, was a source of 'natural' or 'intrinsic' beauty.[2]

Burke made an original contribution which lies outside the main stream of the debate, and was the first to argue that proportion has nothing to do with beauty at all. He agreed that it was determined by both custom and fitness for purpose, and maintained that for that very reason it could not be a cause of beauty: 'If we suppose proportion in natural things to be relative to custom and use, the nature of use and custom will show, that beauty, which is a *positive* and powerful quality, cannot result from it....'[3] Of proportion in works of art he wrote: 'The effects of proportion and fitness, at least so far as they proceed from a mere consideration of the work itself, produce approbation, the acquiescence of the understanding, but not love nor any passion of that species....In beauty, as I said, the effect is previous to any knowledge of the use; but to judge of proportion we must know the end for which any work is designed....'[4]

Hogarth had also supported Berkeley's view that proportion depends on fitness for purpose;[5] later Alison came to the same conclusion, but unlike Burke regarded it at least as a cause of relative beauty: 'I apprehend also, that the beauty of proportion in forms is to be ascribed to this cause; and that certain proportions affect us with the emotion of beauty, not from any original capacity in such qualities to excite this emotion, but from their being expressive to us of the fitness of the parts to the end designed.'[6]

The doctrine of expression enabled him to avoid Burke's objection that the judgment of proportion is an act of understanding. Alison went on to argue that our reactions to the proportions of any object depend on our knowledge of the fitness of its construction, and that 'when any improvement...is made in the construction of the forms of art, so that different proportions of parts are introduced, and produce their end better than the former, the new proportions gradually become beautiful, while the former lose their beauty'.[7]

---

[1] Francis Hutcheson, *An Inquiry into the Original of our Ideas of Beauty and Virtue* (1725), treatise I, III, vii; p. 37 in the 5th edition of 1753.

[2] Lord Kames, *Elements of Criticism*, p. 84 in the 11th edition of 1839.

[3] Edmund Burke, *A Philosophical Enquiry into the Origin of our Ideas of the Sublime and Beautiful* (1756), p. 188 in the edition of 1812.

[4] *Ibid.* pp. 199–200.

[5] William Hogarth, *Analysis of Beauty*, ch. XI.

[6] Alison, *On Taste*, 2nd edition 1811, vol. II, p. 124.   [7] *Ibid.* p. 135.

In Alison's work proportion, though no longer 'a real and independent quality of objects', is at least related to the real fitness of objects for their purpose, if only through our changing knowledge of this fitness. The triumph of subjectivism was still more complete in the theories of Knight, who regarded proportion as an arbitrary convention depending on varying associations of ideas, and therefore not subject to any rules or restrictions.[1]

Architects, meanwhile, had comparatively little to say on the subject of proportion. The earlier philosophers and critics had based their views on material provided in writings on architecture. Not only had Hutcheson taken his views on proportion from Wren, but his celebrated theory of uniformity and variety had been foreshadowed by Sir Henry Wotton.[2] But in the second half of the eighteenth century this was no longer so much the case, and architects contributed little to the debate themselves.

Sir William Chambers still seems to have been very close to Wren's idea of proportion as a source of natural beauty, and he tried to give a qualitative explanation of proportion in architecture as the proper articulation of the parts: 'Perfect proportion...seems to consist in this—that those parts which are either principal or essential should be contrived to catch the eye successively from the most considerable to the least....'[3]

Sir John Soane, however, followed Perrault's distinction between symmetry as a source of 'intrinsic' beauty and proportion as a source of 'relative' beauty, determined not, indeed, by custom, but by 'character' and 'use': 'Beauty is either intrinsic, relative, or compounded of both. Intrinsic beauty determines certain forms and proportions to be beautiful, such as the circle, the polygon, the square, the parallelogram, the cube, the double cube, and others. As no object, strictly speaking, can be relatively beautiful, without reference to use and character, relative beauty therefore determines, amongst other things, the dimensions of doors, windows and chimneys; the length, breadth and rise of the steps of staircases etc....'[4] The characteristic of all the forms determined by 'intrinsic' beauty is symmetry, with the single exception of the double cube. This seems to be an accidental survival of Inigo Jones's application of the musical analogy. Soane's

---

[1] Richard Payne Knight, *An Analytical Inquiry into the Principles of Taste* (1805), pp. 172–6 in the 3rd edition of 1816.

[2] Sir Henry Wotton, *Elements of Architecture*, p. 16 in the facsimile edition of 1903: 'In architecture there may seem to be two opposite affectations, uniformity and variety, which yet will very well suffer a good reconcilement, as we may see in the great pattern of nature, to which I must often resort.' Cf. Francis Hutcheson, *An Inquiry into the Original of our Ideas of Beauty and Virtue*, pp. 17 ff. in the 5th edition of 1753.

[3] Sir William Chambers, *Treatise on Civil Architecture*, p. 138 in the edition of 1862.

[4] Sir John Soane, *Lectures on Architecture*, pp. 113–14 in the edition of 1929.

attitude to the proportions of doors and windows is in complete contrast, for instance, to Wotton's.

For Soane architecture 'has no fixed proportion. Taste, good sense and sound judgment must direct the mind of the architect to apply harmony and justice of relative proportion, the correlation of the parts with the whole, and of the whole with each part.'[1] There is still an echo of Alberti here, but the subjectivist tendencies of Soane's own age are stronger.

(c) SUMMARY AND CONCLUSIONS

Our survey has shown several steps in the argument by means of which the Renaissance theory of proportion was overthrown. The critics first pointed out the weaknesses of the musical analogy. They denied that simply commensurable ratios were pleasing to the eye in themselves, and they went on to deny that any particular relations were pleasing to the eye. In the end they denied that proportion could make an independent contribution to the beauty of objects at all. The importance of proportion was explained as being due to the varying and subjective influences of custom, knowledge of fitness, or a combination of both. The conclusions to be drawn were that proportion was a varying and subjective factor in design, determined by the taste of the individual designer, and that no rules or principles could be established for its control.

The success of this argument lay in the fact that its first steps are entirely justified, and later research has only confirmed them. Thus Helmholtz's study of consonance showed that no exact analogy is possible between musical harmony and architectural proportion. The experiments of Fechner and his successors showed that simply commensurable ratios are not in themselves particularly pleasing to the eye, and they failed to provide very convincing proof that any ratios, even that of the golden section, were pleasing to the eye in themselves.

Once these steps in the argument were accepted, eighteenth-century architects would be left with little to support the view that proportions in a design could be right or wrong in themselves and independently of other considerations. There would only remain the intuitive knowledge that this was true, gained from practical experience of design. To make matters worse the claim that custom and knowledge of fitness determine pleasing proportions is obviously true in part. The pleasing effect of a traditional structure based on the orders may be entirely destroyed if the proportions are very different from those which we are accustomed to expect. In the same way no building is pleasing if its proportions are such that it appears unstable.

[1] Sir John Soane, *Lectures on Architecture*, p. 100 in the edition of 1929.

However, this is not necessarily the whole truth. The requirements of fitness and custom may very well impose certain limits on the proportions of a design. But within these limits proportion may still be free to operate as an independent cause of visual delight. All that is required to reinstate the theory of proportion on these lines is an explanation of how proportion actually works, to take the place of the discarded idea that its beauty is due to the pleasing effect of particular ratios.

This reinstatement was in fact carried out in principle by Barca before the close of the eighteenth century.[1] According to his theory, architectural design was controlled by three factors. The first two, which he called 'construction' and 'imitation', correspond very roughly to 'fitness' and 'custom'. Together these two factors set certain limits to the dimensions of a design. These dimensions were finally fixed within these limits by the third factor, which was 'proportion'.

There were two rules of proportion, of which the first was the use of simply commensurable ratios. This is the least original part of Barca's system; but even so the use of simply commensurable ratios, which were supposed to be easily recognized, was treated merely as a means to an end. The second and most important rule of proportion was that of the repetition of ratios, which implies the repetition of similar shapes. This idea had been foreshadowed by various Renaissance writers. Hutcheson had spoken of uniformity of proportion as the foundation of the beauty of works of art.[2] But the first clear and explicit statement of the principle is Barca's.

Barca explained the importance of uniformity of ratios in terms of the unity which it can produce in a design: 'There cannot be beauty or proportion in the whole without unity, which cannot be obtained otherwise than with uniformity of ratios or divisions in all the separate parts.'[3] In the application of his theory to the orders, which occupies a large part of his book, he shows how the repetition of ratios can be carried out in practice.[4]

But it is doubtful whether Barca's theory had much immediate effect. The tide of subjectivism was flowing strongly, and the fact that Barca retained the use of simply commensurable ratios may well have concealed the originality of his ideas. It was not until much later in the nineteenth century that the repetition of ratios reappeared, and then in a very different form.

[1] Barca's essay, *Proporzione in architettura*, although not published until 1806, was based on lectures given in the Academy of Sciences in Padua from 1793 to 1798.

[2] Francis Hutcheson, *An Inquiry into the Original of our Ideas of Beauty and Virtue*, 5th edition 1753, treatise 1, pp. 37–8.

[3] Barca, *Proporzione in architettura*, p. 23. The Italian runs as follows: '...non può esservi Bello o proporzione nel tutto senza un' unità, la quale non si può ottenere altrimenti, che colla uniformità di ragioni o divisioni in tutte le particolari composizioni.'

[4] See, for example, his Corinthian order reproduced in Plate 12, where the subdivision 3 : 2 : 2 is repeated five times in the proportions of the capital and entablature.

Meanwhile the collapse of the theory of proportion left architectural theory in a state of confusion whose results are still apparent. In one way, however, this disintegration was not without advantages. It provided the theory of architecture with a kind of pupal phase in which all its ideas could be taken to pieces and re-examined. In the field of proportion the minority who were still interested in an objective theory of proportion could introduce new ideas, and break away from the concentration on commensurable ratios. The revivals brought an interest in other types of proportion, and prepared the way for a broader theory in which commensurable and incommensurable ratios are alike merely means to an end.

CHAPTER V

THE RETURN TO
THE INCOMMENSURABLE (1)

THE REVIVALS

(A) INTRODUCTION

The collapse of the Renaissance theory of architecture, and of the theory of proportion which formed part of it, left the architects and builders of nineteenth-century England to face the largest building programme the world had yet seen without any coherent intellectual principles to guide them. The results of this disaster are obvious to our eyes. What requires explaining is not, perhaps, that many buildings of nineteenth-century England are bad, but that any of them are good.

As far as the theory of proportion was concerned, we have seen how the critical and experimental approach of the early Renaissance had failed to achieve the same success as it had in other fields, and how the theory which did come to be accepted was already recognized as inadequate in the eighteenth century. This failure of established theory left two alternatives. The first was not merely to do without theory, but to deny the relevance of reasoned theory to the problem of proportion, which became a matter of personal intuition. This attitude reflected the romantic individualism so strong in the literary movements of the period. In the absence of any convincing theory it was inevitably adopted in practice by the majority of architects, and is common today.

The second alternative was to try to formulate a new theory of proportion from first principles. This task was undertaken by a small minority of enthusiasts who were not afraid of the charge of charlatanry which has sometimes been made. Their attitude reflected the scientific tendencies of the nineteenth century, and was in opposition to the disastrous and rapidly growing gulf between art and science. Odd though some of their theories appear to us, it is as a result of their work that we are able to formulate a more satisfactory theory today. It is for this reason that an outline of some of the nineteenth-century theories must be given.

Ruskin is usually regarded as a spokesman of the intuitive school, and it was no doubt this side of his work which was most heeded by his readers. In *Modern Painters* he told them that ' it is utterly vain to endeavour to reduce this proportion to finite rules, for it is as various as musical melody, and the laws to which it is subject are of the same general kind; so that the determination of right or wrong proportion is as much a matter of feeling and experience as the appreciation of good musical composition'.[1]

The emphasis on feeling shows us Ruskin as a romantic individualist, but the objection to finite rules and the stress on the infinite possibilities of proportion need not mean anything more than the rejection of arbitrary numerical rules for the proportions of the orders. Twenty years later, Viollet-le-Duc was to use very similar words in condemning 'fixed proportions, constantly the same', and in advocating the 'infinitely varied application of the laws of geometry'.[2]

Ruskin did, as a matter of fact, make an extremely important positive contribution to the theory of proportion in his clear distinction between 'apparent' proportion, 'the sensible relation of qualities', and 'constructive' proportion, 'the adaptation of quantities to functions'. 'Apparent proportion' is 'one of the most important means of obtaining unity amongst things which otherwise must have remained distinct', and 'may be considered as lying at the root of most of our impressions of the beautiful'. 'Constructive proportion', on the other hand, 'is agreeable, not (necessarily) to the eye, but to the mind, which is cognizant of the function to be performed'.[3]

How little effect this side of Ruskin's work had is shown by the fact that it had to be repeated independently by Nobbs, who makes a similar clear distinction between 'formal' and 'functional' proportion,[4] and whose valuable work on the effect of size on 'constructive' or 'functional' proportion was also anticipated in some measure by Ruskin. And yet it is natural that Ruskin's genuine contribution to the theory of proportion escaped attention: in the preface to the second edition of *Seven Lamps of Architecture*, the book in which one would naturally look for a theory of proportion, he disparages proportion in architecture, comparing it to 'the disposition of dishes at a dinner-table, of ornaments on a dress'.[5]

Most of the work on architectural proportion in the nineteenth century was stimulated by the archaeological study of Greek and Gothic buildings associated with the revivals: in spite of the destructive criticism which the Renaissance theory had been given, there remained a lingering feeling in many people's minds that if Renaissance architects had failed to solve the problem of proportion, Greek or Gothic architects might have held the key to its solution. At the same time,

[1] *Modern Painters*, vol. II (1846), p. 66 in the edition of 1898.
[2] *Dictionnaire raisonné de l'architecture française du XIe au XVIe siècle* (1854–68), vol. VII, pp. 532, 534.
[3] *Modern Painters*, vol. II, p. 62.
[4] *Design: a Treatise on the Discovery of Form* (1937).
[5] *Seven Lamps of Architecture*, p. xxvi.

protests were made against the prevailing habit of merely copying ancient architecture, instead of mastering its principles and applying them afresh to present-day problems.

Billings, a Gothic revivalist, protested as follows: 'The more we examine the powers of Design developed by the aid of *fixed diagrams*, or foundations, the more absurd does it appear, that ever since the revival of Gothic architecture we should have gone on for ever copying—taking it for granted as a preliminary that all possible combinations were exhibited in the works of our predecessors; considering, in short, that the mine was exhausted....'[1]

Hay believed that a science of proportion was known to the Greeks. He described the orders as 'so perfect that, since the science which gave them birth has been buried in oblivion, classical architecture has been little more than an imitative art'.[2]

This archaeological interest in proportion was no doubt confined to a minority of theorists, and had little direct influence on architectural practice. Moreover, these theorists were not working within an accepted framework of established theory, like the writers of the seventeenth and eighteenth centuries; they were trying to recover what they believed to be a lost science of the past by speculation based on the most slender evidence, and some of their theories may well seem to us to have been the wildest guesses. It would be easy to dismiss their work as unimportant, but this would be a mistake. The theories of proportion associated with the revivals are of value, not for any flickering light they may throw on the methods of Greek and Gothic architects, but as a necessary transitional phase between the eighteenth century and the present.

The Renaissance theory of proportion had degenerated into a narrow and inflexible theory based on arithmetic and the use of simply commensurable ratios. It had been developed as far as was possible in this direction, and some sort of fresh start on a broader basis had become necessary. We can now see that this is just what the nineteenth century provided. The structure of the old theory was broken down, and a pupal phase followed in which the old material was shaped into a new form.

The most significant thing about this process of renovation was the shift of interest from arithmetic and the analytical study of linear proportions to geometry and the study of shape. This automatically freed proportional theory from its restriction to simply commensurable ratios, and encouraged the growth of interest in the incommensurable. It was only in this way that it eventually became possible to return to a more completely analytical theory, which included the incommensurable as well as the commensurable.

Of the theories of proportion associated with the revivals, the 'Gothic' theory was geometrical from the start. The 'Greek' theory was handicapped by the respect

[1] R. W. Billings, *The Power of Form applied to Geometric Tracery* (1851), p. 9.
[2] D. R. Hay, *The Science of Beauty as developed in Nature and applied in Art* (Edinburgh, 1856), p. 36.

still felt for Vitruvius, and it was some time before the attempt to interpret Greek architecture in terms of simply commensurable ratios was abandoned. But in spite of this it will be more convenient to give an account of Gothic theory first, as the Greek theory affords a better introduction to later theory, especially that of Hambidge.[1] As far as the theories of Greece and of the Middle Ages themselves are concerned, we shall have to discuss some of the fragments of indirect literary evidence which survive. We shall not, however, attempt any elaborate reconstruction of ancient theory ourselves.

(B) THE GOTHIC PERIOD

(i) *Literary evidence surviving from the Middle Ages.* The theorists of the Gothic revival did their best to accumulate all the available literary evidence on the subject of medieval theories of proportion. The results of this labour were very slight, and can quickly be summarized here.

Some of the indirect evidence should be mentioned first. Aquinas, the great figure of thirteenth-century philosophy and interpreter of Aristotle, inherited from Greece and from St Augustine an objective theory of beauty. In the *Summa Theologica* he several times refers to proportion as an element of beauty.[2] While he naturally does not go into technical details, his remarks suggest that a medieval architect might be expected to take the subject of proportion very seriously.

Even more important clues are provided by the history of mathematical studies. From the twelfth century onwards translations of Euclid from the Arabic began to appear, and the love of geometry which this stimulated was clearly expressed in architecture. The relevance of Euclid's mathematical theory of proportion to the problem of architectural proportion must have been far from obvious, but what architects did learn from Euclid was geometrical construction and the manipulation of geometrical figures. They did not, for instance, need to go very far to construct an equilateral triangle, by a method which uses the famous figure of the vesica piscis.[3]

Little original work was done by medieval mathematicians, who had first to

---

[1] Although a distinction between 'Gothic' and 'Greek' theory is necessary, it cannot always be applied to the theorists themselves. Thus Cockerell and Penrose studied the proportions of both Greek and Gothic buildings.

[2] E.g. 'For beauty there are three requirements. First, a certain wholeness or perfection, for whatever is incomplete is, so far, ugly; second, a due proportion or harmony; and third, clarity, so that brightly coloured things are called beautiful' (I, xxxix, 8).

'The beauty of the body consists in a man having his bodily members well proportioned, together with a certain appropriate clarity of colour' (II (2), cxlv, 2). These translations are from E. F. Carritt's *Philosophies of Beauty* (1931).

[3] 'Elements', book I, proposition I.

assimilate what they had learnt from Euclid and the Arabs. An exception was provided by Leonardo of Pisa, after whom the Fibonacci series was named. Less important mathematically, but of importance to us for its obvious application to the Gothic rose window, and for its possible application in what is more strictly the field of proportion, is the work of Bradwardine on star polygons.[1] Amongst more direct evidence of the application of mathematics to art in the Middle Ages, the sketch-book of Willard de Honnecourt is often cited. While this shows the interest in geometry which might be expected, it throws little light on the use to which geometry was put.

Interest in Gothic systems of proportion was encouraged by the report, made in 1321, on the extension of Siena Cathedral; this condemns the alteration because the existing building was 'so justly proportioned, and its members so well agreed with each other in breadth, length and height, that if in any part an addition were made to it...the whole would be destroyed'. This might easily have been written by Alberti, and, in the words of the *Encyclopaedia of Architecture*, it 'would seem to prove that some system had existed'.[2]

A more specific reference to proportional theory occurs in the account of the dispute over the design of Milan Cathedral in 1392, when a majority of architects were in favour of carrying out the design 'non al quadrato, ma fino al triangolo'.[3] Much importance was later to be attached to this statement by Macody Lund, who named his work on proportion *Ad Quadratum*.

The reference to the triangle in the Milan discussions seems to be explained by the account of Gothic principles of design given by Cesariano in the commentary to his translation of Vitruvius. Although this was published in 1521, and is therefore very far from being a contemporary document, it was evidently based on what was still remembered of these principles, which Cesariano described as the 'rule of the German architects'. It is of great importance as the only clear account of Gothic methods which has survived.

Cesariano mentioned three rules for designing churches. The first fixed the overall length and breadth of the church by means of the vesica piscis, the second provided for the subdivision of the plan into equal bays, and the third determined the

[1] Noted by Macody Lund in *Ad Quadratum*, i, pp. 29, 141.

[2] Gwilt's *Encyclopaedia of Architecture* (1881), p. 966. The original edition of 1842 was expanded after Gwilt's death by the incorporation of new material, especially by the addition in 1867 of Edward Cresy's articles on proportion which were originally included in his own *Encyclopaedia of Civil Engineering* (1861). The book was revised by Wyatt Papworth in 1881, and provides a mine of information on nineteenth-century theories of proportion.

[3] *Ibid.* p. 966. Extracts from the cathedral records were presented to the Royal Institute of British Architects in 1854 by J. W. Papworth.

heights of the various parts by means of equilateral triangles.[1] It is these rules which were the justification for the many nineteenth-century attempts to reconstruct a Gothic system of proportion based on the equilateral triangle, or on the related figure of the vesica piscis. They inspired research like Cockerell's work on Wykeham's chapels at Oxford and Winchester,[2] and Penrose's study of Lincoln Cathedral,[3] which afforded some confirmation of the use of the rules. But in neither case was it proved that all three rules had been observed.

While the reference to the use of the equilateral triangle in section and of the vesica piscis in plan is of interest, the use of the vesica piscis may in fact have been nothing more than a convenient method of setting out the main axes of the building at right angles to each other. Several sixteenth-century writers, including Cesariano himself, appear to have recommended its use precisely for this purpose.[4]

The evidence we have summarized here does suggest that medieval architects were keenly interested in geometry and in its application to the problem of proportion in the widest sense of the word. But it is doubtful whether this interest got beyond the formulation of arbitrary rules for the setting-out of the general lines of buildings on the one hand, and the exploration of the symmetry of geometrical form and pattern on the other hand.

There is much to be said for the view that Gothic architects were simply feeling their way towards a genuine theory of proportion in the narrower sense, which appears in their work in an embryonic form in the repetition of simple geometrical figures such as the equilateral triangle. This seems to be Hambidge's view,[5] though Macody Lund believed that real Gothic achievements in proportion were brought to an end by the 'decline of intellectualism' following the Black Death.[6] We are not, however, concerned directly with this problem, but rather with the lines of thought which its study suggested to nineteenth-century theorists.

(ii) *Theorists of the Gothic revival.* No attempt can be made here to give a detailed account of nineteenth-century research into the problem of Gothic proportion, but some examples will be given of the kind of theories which were elaborated.

In England interest in the subject developed gradually at first, and by the middle of the century papers on the subject were often being read to bodies like the Royal Institute of British Architects and the Archaeological Institute.[7] An early study

---

[1] *Encyclopaedia of Architecture*, pp. 966 and 971. The rules are contained in fos. xiv and xv of Cesariano's commentary. Professor Ghyka reproduces an extremely interesting diagram illustrating the application of the third rule to the design of Milan Cathedral in his *Geometry of Art and Life*, p. 151.

[2] *Encyclopaedia of Architecture*, p. 965.   [3] *Ibid.* p. 974.

[4] *Ibid.* p. 968. The other writers mentioned are Caporali, 1536, and Delorme, 1576.

[5] Jay Hambidge, *Dynamic Symmetry* (1920), p. 140.   [6] F. Macody Lund, *Ad Quadratum*, I, p. 71.

[7] The work of this period is summed up in the *Encyclopaedia of Architecture*.

of this type is that of Kerrich, who read a paper on the use of the vesica piscis in Gothic architecture to the Society of Antiquaries in 1820.[1] Cockerell was later to accuse Kerrich of concealing his debt to Cesariano,[2] but as Kerrich's use of the vesica is very different from Cesariano's, the accusation is perhaps unfounded. Indeed, Kerrich would be unlikely to suppress any evidence which would give credit to his own theory, and he does in fact refer to the use of the vesica by Dürer.

Kerrich's work seems to be entirely original. On finding that the normal vesica piscis was not enough to explain all the forms of Gothic architecture, he proceeded to invent a series of them. He divided the shorter diameter of the normal vesica piscis into twelve equal parts, and used these divisions as centres for five new vesicas and a circle. These six different forms of the vesica piscis and the circle define the shapes of six different rectangles and the square which contain them.

Armed with this battery of rectangles, Kerrich was highly successful in analysing Gothic architecture, and made the sweeping claim that 'all the seven rectangles...I have found actually used for the plans of Choirs, Chancels, Chapels, Porches, etc. in Norman and Gothic buildings, one only excepted; and I have met with no plans of such buildings that did not agree with one or other of them'.[3] But in spite of this he felt the need of a further set of rectangles in carrying out his analyses.

It is very easy to reject this scheme as absurd. Nobbs speaks of archaeologists who 'have sought among the ruins of Greece and of Rome with circles and squares and other figures; and they have found some analogies of form and invented others'.[4] In Kerrich's study of Gothic architecture, the process of invention is not concealed. Having provided himself by an entirely arbitrary process with a wide enough range of rectangles, he only needs what Nobbs calls a 'little selective adroitness'[5] to apply them to the small-scale drawings with which his paper is profusely illustrated.

As a serious study of Gothic architecture, Kerrich's work has obvious weaknesses, but as a contribution to the development of proportional theory it has two features of interest. The first is the stress on the rectangle, and the use of a series or scale of rectangles of different shapes, defined not arithmetically, like Alberti's recommended shapes for rooms, but geometrically. The idea reappears in the equally eccentric work of Hay,[6] and later becomes part of the solid structure of proportional theory in the work of Hambidge, Harry Roberts, and Corbusier.

The second feature of interest lies in the actual character of these geometrically defined rectangles. The ratio of the sides of the rectangle defined by the normal

[1] *Archaeologia*, XIX (1821), pp. 353–68.   [2] *Encyclopaedia of Architecture*, p. 971.
[3] *Archaeologia*, XIX (1821), p. 354.
[4] *Design: a Treatise on the Discovery of Form*, p. 134.   [5] *Ibid*. p. 131.
[6] *The Science of Beauty as developed in Nature and applied in Art*.

vesica piscis is $\sqrt{3}:1$, and that of the square is of course $1:1$. The ratios of the sides of Kerrich's intermediate rectangles are:[1]

$$2\sqrt{2}:\sqrt{3}, \quad \sqrt{7}:\sqrt{3}, \quad \sqrt{2}:1, \quad \sqrt{5}:\sqrt{3} \quad \text{and} \quad 2:\sqrt{3}.$$

This affords a good illustration of the immediate effect of geometrical methods in restoring the importance of incommensurable ratios. It is also of interest that two of Kerrich's rectangles are simple root-rectangles.

An example of work which is possibly based on more solid foundations is Cresy's essay on Stone Church. Cresy describes the revival of geometry in the twelfth century, and its effect on architecture. He speaks of the disappearance of the round arch, and the emergence of a 'new style altogether, having principles essentially geometrical; and it is vain that we attempt to imitate the tracery or mouldings belonging to this style correctly, unless we consider them to emanate from some simple figure. However numerous the mouldings, they never appear confused....'[2] He goes on to show the importance of the related figures of the equilateral triangle, the hexagon, and the dodecagon in Gothic architecture up to the beginning of the fifteenth century, when the system 'underwent a great and important change by the introduction of the isosceles triangle and its compound the pentagon'.

Cresy's insistence on the use of dominant geometrical figures seems to contain the germ of Thiersch's principle of analogy; and his account of the historical development of the use of geometrical forms foreshadows several later accounts. White, for instance, considers that the square and equilateral triangle were used in the Norman period, that later the square dropped out, and that in the middle of the fourteenth century a system of diagonal squares was adopted.[3] All of this has probably more to do with symmetry than with what we have agreed to call proportion in the narrower sense, although the appearance of the pentagon has persuaded some later writers to attribute an interest in the golden section to the later Middle Ages, and it has assumed considerable importance in the work of Macody Lund.

Cresy expressed his opposition to the subjectivism of his period as follows: '...it is to the neglect of the application of the rules of geometry that we may attribute the defects and failures wherever an imitation of this early style has been attempted in the present day, which neglect has been greatly fostered by the too

---

[1] The relationship between the seven ratios can best be shown by putting them in the following form:

$$\frac{\sqrt{9}}{\sqrt{3}} \quad \frac{\sqrt{8}}{\sqrt{3}} \quad \frac{\sqrt{7}}{\sqrt{3}} \quad \frac{\sqrt{6}}{\sqrt{3}} \quad \frac{\sqrt{5}}{\sqrt{3}} \quad \frac{\sqrt{4}}{\sqrt{3}} \quad \frac{\sqrt{3}}{\sqrt{3}}$$

[2] *Illustrations of Stone Church, Kent* (1840), p. 5.

[3] Article in the *Ecclesiologist* (1853). The transition from square to equilateral triangle and back to diagonal square reappears in Klein's *Science and the Infinite* (1921).

prevailing opinion that all the beauty we admire is produced by art alone unaided by the science of geometry....'[1]

It is not necessary to give a detailed analysis here of the work of other writers like Chantrell,[2] Griffith[3] or Henszlmann,[4] but before we leave the Gothic revival some account must be given of the work of the French writer Viollet-le-Duc, whose contribution is based on an unrivalled knowledge of the Gothic architecture of France, and, coming in the second half of the nineteenth century, shows a maturity which earlier work sometimes lacked.

His analysis of Gothic proportions is based on the use of three different kinds of triangle: the right-angled isosceles triangle, the familiar equilateral triangle, and what he calls the 'Egyptian' triangle, an isosceles triangle with a height of $2\frac{1}{2}$ parts compared to a base of 4 parts. The use of the first two of these in design is more or less equivalent to the use of $45°$ and $30°–60°$ set-squares, a fact which is apparent in many of Viollet-le-Duc's illustrations. This system of proportion tends to generate the triple geometric progression based on the numbers $\sqrt{3}$, $1 + \sqrt{3}$, and 2 as its characteristic pattern of proportional relationships.

In trying to justify the stress on the triangle in medieval architecture Viollet-le-Duc seems to have fallen into the mistake of confusing 'formal' and 'functional' proportion: 'Les proportions en architecture s'établissent d'abord sur les lois de la stabilité, et les lois de la stabilité dérivent de la géométrie. Un triangle est une figure ...parfaite, en ce qu'elle donne l'idée la plus exacte de la stabilité.'[5]

We have already seen that like Ruskin he objected to the fixed proportions of the Renaissance, but saw no difficulty in the use of variable proportions based on mathematics: '...l'architecture n'est pas l'esclave d'un système hiératique de proportions, mais au contraire peut se modifier sans cesse et trouver des applications toujours nouvelles, des rapports proportionnels, aussi bien qu'elle trouve des applications variées à l'infini des lois de la géométrie.'[6] Also like Ruskin he was careful to distinguish between proportion and symmetry, a word which he kept to the strict sense of bilateral symmetry, and he commented almost prophetically on the dangers of confusing the two words.

The comparison with Ruskin cannot, however, be carried very far, as Viollet-le-Duc was more consistently scientific in his attitude to architecture, and condemned the purely subjective unequivocally: 'Un malheur aujourd'hui dans les arts, et particulièrement dans l'architecture, c'est de croire que l'on peut pratiquer cet art

---

[1] *Illustrations of Stone Church, Kent*, pp. 5–6.
[2] Paper read to the R.I.B.A. in 1847 and published in the *Builder*.
[3] *Natural System of Architecture* (1845). Other works are listed in the R.I.B.A. library catalogue.
[4] Paper read to the R.I.B.A. in 1852.
[5] *Dictionnaire raisonné*, article on proportion, vol. VII, p. 534.   [6] *Ibid.*

sous l'inspiration de la pure fantaisie, et qu'on élève un monument avec cette donnée très vague qu'on veut appeler le goût, comme on compose une toilette de femme....'[1]

Of the greatest interest is the historical comparison between Greek architecture, with no visible relationship between the proportions of the interior and those of the exterior, Roman and Byzantine architecture, where the exterior was the exact envelope of the structure of the interior, and Gothic architecture, which combined the Greek sensitiveness to proportion with the Roman method of working outwards from the internal structure of the building. It is this theory, that 'it is the harmonic system used for the interior which determines the visible proportions of the exterior', which Macody Lund made the basis of his study of proportion.[2]

Viollet-le-Duc's language foreshadows that of today in many respects. His phrases 'système harmonique' and 'échelle harmonique' seem to anticipate Professor Ghyka. The description of geometrical figures as 'générateurs de proportions' prepares us for Corbusier's 'tracés régulateurs', and in stressing the importance of the human scale he was also preparing the way for Corbusier.

Finally, although he was himself mainly interested in the geometrical systems of the Middle Ages, Viollet-le-Duc was prepared to recognize the value of other mathematical treatments of the problem of proportion. He made the important distinction between systems of proportion based on arithmetic and systems based on geometry: '...il est impossible à tout praticien de concevoir et de développer un système harmonique sans avoir recours aux figures géométriques ou à l'arithmétique....'[3] '...Les architectes de l'antiquité ont suivi les formules arithmétiques dans la composition de leurs ordres, des rapports de nombres, tandis que les architectes du moyen âge se sont servis des triangles pour obtenir des rapports harmoniques.'[4]

In attributing an arithmetical system to the Greeks as well as to the Romans, Viollet-le-Duc relied on the work of Aurès, who had tried to avoid the difficulties into which this theory was beginning to run by taking measurements half-way up his columns instead of at the bottom.[5]

We can now turn to a consideration of 'Greek' theory in the nineteenth century, since, although our survey of 'Gothic' theory has been by no means exhaustive, it has brought out the ideas of permanent value which were contributed.

---

[1] *Dictionnaire raisonné*, vol. VII, p. 550.

[2] Quoted in translation in *Ad Quadratum*, I, pp. 1–2. Viollet-le-Duc's remark, 'c'est le système harmonique admis pour l'intérieur qui a commandé les proportions visibles à l'extérieur' (*Dictionnaire raisonné*, p. 538), refers specifically to Roman and Byzantine architecture. Of Gothic architecture he says: '...dans l'architecture du moyen âge le système harmonique des proportions procède du dedans au dehors...' (p. 537).

[3] *Dictionnaire raisonné*, vol. VII, p. 550.   [4] *Ibid.* p. 536.

[5] *Nouvelle théorie du module* (1862).

(C) GREECE

It would be inappropriate to state at this point the indirect literary evidence as to the nature of theories of architectural proportion in Greece. There is plenty of material of this nature, both philosophical and mathematical, but its importance has only been realized fairly recently. We are concerned at present with the theorists of the nineteenth century, and they believed that they possessed direct evidence in the work of Vitruvius. Our immediate task is to trace their disillusionment.

Growing interest in Greek architecture had led to a realization of his Hellenistic sympathies, and his work was studied again in the belief that it would throw light on the design of classical Greek as well as of Greco-Roman architecture. Wilkins justified his new translation of parts of Vitruvius[1] by the claim that he had been able to correct the mistakes of earlier editors and translators, who had approached the problem of interpreting the book from the point of view of Roman rather than Greek building practice. This translation was naturally one that would recommend itself to students of Greek architecture, and it was studied and quoted not only by nineteenth-century writers like Hay,[2] but much more recently and from a very different point of view by Hambidge.[3]

It is therefore interesting to find that Wilkins goes a great deal further than other translators in making Vitruvius an advocate of the desirability of commensurable proportions.[4] He could hardly have done this from a knowledge of Greek practice, but the special emphasis which he gave to the importance of commensurability may well have helped to determine the direction of research into the proportions of Greek buildings.

An early nineteenth-century writer on architectural theory was Legh, whose work shows a marked departure from the more cautious approach, rooted in tradition, of the previous period. He attempted an ambitious reconstruction of what he imagined a Greek theory of architecture might have been, using the terminology of Vitruvius: '...having been thoroughly convinced, that the Greeks were governed by principles of which we know nothing, and conceiving it very possible that the incoherent

---

[1] William Wilkins, *The Civil Architecture of Vitruvius* (1812).

[2] D. R. Hay, *The Science of Beauty* .

[3] Jay Hambidge, *Dynamic Symmetry*. Hambidge quotes at length from Wilkins's translation on p. 9.

[4] E.g. 'Proportion is the commensuration of the various constituent parts with the whole...' (III, i, 1). '...The component parts of sacred edifices ought to be commensurate with each other...' (III, i, 2). '...The human frame appears to have been formed with such propriety that the several members are commensurate with the whole' (III, i, 4). '...Those are entitled to our commendation who, in building temples to their deities, proportioned the edifices so that the several parts of them might be commensurate with the whole' (III, i, 9). The usual book and chapter numbering is given here to facilitate comparison with other versions, although Wilkins numbered his shortened version rather differently.

string of terms used in the second chapter of Vitruvius, which nobody has ever been able to explain, may, perhaps, be the only existing remnant of those principles and ancient theories, I have ventured to hope to succeed in interpreting and engrafting them in the following essays.'[1] In proportion Legh was an advocate of simple commensurability.

The archaeologists themselves, who by their published measurements of Greek buildings supplied the material for the proportional theorists to work on, can be represented by Penrose and Cockerell. Penrose believed that 'in the Parthenon most of the principal dimensions are aliquot parts of one another, the common measures being generally low numbers'.[2] His description of the Parthenon includes, however, few references to commensurable ratios, and those which occur are neither very simple nor do they always correspond very accurately to his measurements. Ratios like 7:12 and 6:25 occur, and there is the following interesting case of a repetition of ratios:

$$\frac{\text{Height from top step}}{\text{Breadth of top step}} = \frac{\text{Height of columns}}{\text{Height from top step}} = \frac{7}{12}.$$

The first of the ratios between the actual measurements does approximate closely to 7:12, but the second falls short by an error of about 1%. This error may be regarded as trivial, for it would not be apparent to the eye. It is, however, a fact that the average of the two ratios is actually closer either to $\phi^2 : 2\sqrt{5}$ or to $\sqrt{2}:\theta$, so an 'incommensurable' interpretation of the ratios is quite as possible as Penrose's own 'commensurable' interpretation.

Cockerell included in his published work on certain Greek temples[3] an important memoir on proportion by William Watkyss Lloyd. Lloyd adopted the view, for which he claimed abundant proof, 'that the Greek architects attached great value to simple ratios of low natural numbers for regulating the proportions of parts and divisions of their structures relatively to each other'.[4] He analysed the proportions of the temples which Cockerell had measured in terms of this theory, and was most successful in the case of the temple at Bassae. Here he had no difficulty in discovering simply commensurable ratios, and gave a complete analysis of the Ionic order of the interior of the naos based on the ratios 1:1, 2:1 and 3:1. But the method of arithmetical analysis, unlike the geometrical analysis used by students of Gothic proportions, clearly shows the degree of accuracy attained. Unfortunately,

[1] P. Legh, *Music of the Eye*, p. 20.

[2] Penrose, *Athenian Architecture* (1851), p. 78.

[3] C. R. Cockerell, *The Temples of Jupiter Panhellenius at Aegina and of Apollo Epicurius at Bassae* (1860), containing W. W. Lloyd's 'Memoir of the systems of proportion employed in the design of the Doric temples at Phigaleia and Aegina.'   [4] *Ibid.* p. 63.

Lloyd was most successful in discovering simple ratios where he was prepared to accept rather a high margin of error.

There were, however, elements of the greatest value in Lloyd's work. These were his independent discovery of the *principle of the repetition of ratios*, which had been stated already by Barca, and his recognition of the fact that it was the repetition itself which was important, rather than the nature of the ratios which were repeated. The principle is explained in his preliminary discussion of Greek proportion: 'The ratios employed in a particular building are comparatively few, being selected with reference to the forms required, their contrasts and gradations. Hence certain leading ratios are repeated and varied in mode of application; they are never applied without logical propriety, and above all the harmony of proportion is consulted by persistent selection of rectilinear proportions that conciliate rect-angular and vice versa.'[1] Of the scheme of proportions for the order of the naos of the temple at Bassae, he says that 'the unity and variety of effect obtained with such conspicuous economy of ratio, are worthy of all admiration'.[2]

Here is a link between the aesthetic principle of unity and variety established by Hutcheson in the early eighteenth century on foundations laid by Wotton and Wren, and the proportional theory of today. Whether Lloyd was in fact rediscovering a principle known to the Greeks, or merely attributing to them one which he had invented himself, there can be no question of the value of his work in giving the principle of the repetition of ratios what seems to be its first clear statement in English architectural literature.

The difficulty of interpreting the proportions of Greek buildings accurately in terms of simply commensurable ratios had already led to other explanations of them, in which we can see the growing interest in geometry as opposed to arithmetic. The publication of John Pennethorne's main work on Greek architecture was de-layed until much later,[3] but his *Elements and Mathematical Principles of the Greek Architects and Artists* appeared in 1844. Pennethorne believed that mathematics and art were closely linked in Greece, and suggested that it was art which provided the stimulus for mathematical studies in Greece, in the way in which science provided it in modern Europe.[4] This idea becomes still more important in the light of Hambidge's work on the use of the 'application of areas' in Greek art as well as in geometry.[5]

[1] C. R. Cockerell, *The Temples of Jupiter Panhellenius at Aegina and of Apollo Epicurius at Bassae*, p. 64.

[2] *Ibid.* p. 77.   [3] *Geometry and Optics of Ancient Architecture* (1878).

[4] *Elements and Mathematical Principles* (1844), p. 9.

[5] 'For the purpose of dividing up the areas of rectangles so that the divisions would be recognizable, the Greeks had recourse to a simple but ingenious method which is called the "application of areas". This idea was used by them both in science and in art' (Jay Hambidge, *Elements of Dynamic Symmetry* (1948 edition), p. 28.

Pennethorne's work on the subtle optical corrections of Greek architecture is well known. In the field of proportion he regarded the deviations from perfect commensurability as an example of another kind of optical correction. He believed that Greek buildings were designed in the first place with their dimensions commensurable, and that these were then modified to correct the distortions due to perspective. The two operations were identified with Vitruvius' 'ordinatio' and 'eurythmia', and the necessary calculations with 'dispositio'.[1] What Pennethorne was in fact suggesting was that the dimensions of Greek buildings were made commensurable, not in their length, but in the angle of sight which they subtend at the eye. In this case everything would of course depend on the choice of view-point.

Another writer who rejected the idea of commensurability of linear dimensions, but who could not free himself completely from commensurability, was Hay, who invented an entirely original form of the musical analogy. Hay did not believe that the eye was interested in the numerical ratio between the sides of the rectangle. But he noticed that it was able accurately to judge the direction of lines, and came to the conclusion that 'angles of direction must all bear to some fixed angle the same simple relations which the different notes in a chord of music bear to the fundamental note'.[2]

Applied to the rectangle this meant that the diagonals had to divide the right angles between the sides into commensurable parts. Here we have a change from the methods of arithmetic to those of geometry. By providing himself with a kind of scale of rectangles of this type, Hay was able to analyse to his own satisfaction the proportions of the Parthenon, the human figure, and the Greek vase.

The interest of this extraordinary system lies in the fact that the change to geometry immediately introduced incommensurability of dimension, even if commensurability was preserved amongst the angles. Just as in Kerrich's very different but equally artificial system, the root-rectangles and rectangles related to them began to appear. Thus the $\sqrt{3}$ rectangle has its diagonals at $30°$ and $60°$ to its sides, and for the θ rectangle these angles become $22\frac{1}{2}°$ and $67\frac{1}{2}°$, or $\frac{1}{4}$ and $\frac{3}{4}$ of a right angle. This is not of course an argument in favour of eccentric systems like those of Kerrich and Hay, but it shows how they took their place in preparing the ground for later discoveries. Hambidge, for instance, was well aware of Hay's interest in root-rectangles.[3]

A very different approach to the problem of proportion was made by Gwilt. His own system of planning by means of a grid of squares,[4] borrowed from the French

[1] *Elements and Mathematical Principles*, p. 19.
[2] *The Science of Beauty*, p. 37.   [3] *Dynamic Symmetry*, p. 145.
[4] *Rudiments of Architecture*, pp. 144–6 in the second edition of 1839. Also *Encyclopaedia of Architecture* (1842), p. 893 in the edition of 1881.

writer Durand,[1] represents the translation of the use of simply commensurable ratios from arithmetic into geometry, and foreshadows much present-day 'modular planning'. His approach to the problem of Greek proportion is quite distinct, and is based on the work of Lebrun.[2] The confusion between 'formal' and 'functional' proportion is considerable in Gwilt's writing, but in connexion with Greek proportion he followed those eighteenth-century writers who identified proportion with fitness. 'The laws of statics, though not perhaps in the earliest periods so well understood as now, were nevertheless so intuitively felt as to guide the first architects in their proportions....'[3] The principle of proportion which Gwilt put forward, 'that no support should be burthened with a greater quantity of matter than itself contains', may well seem to us rather an impostor amongst the laws of statics, but it does appear to give a rough guide to Greek building practice.[4]

In practice the area of the pediment and entablature of the building was compared to the area, in elevation, of the columns supporting them. The idea was developed by Cresy, who combined it with an analysis of the elevation of the building by means of squares.[5] The well-known and rather mysterious drawings of Doric orders in Sir Banister Fletcher's *History of Architecture*[6] are examples of Cresy's type of analysis. Their significance lies not merely in the use of the squares, but in the fact that the areas of the load, or entablature and pediment, the supports, or columns, and the voids, or area between the columns, are all equal. The same principle was applied by Cresy to the other orders, and he considered that the only difference lay in the fact that the voids occupied half the total area instead of a third.

No claim for great accuracy was made on behalf of this system. It is rather outside the scope of our present discussion, but is of interest as a rare example of the study of what we have described as the third relationship of visual proportion, that of objects having the same area but different shapes.[7]

(D) CONCLUSION

Our study of the nineteenth-century attempts to rediscover the proportional systems of the past has disclosed two methods of analysing archaeological material. The first method, that of the numerical analysis of the actual linear measurements,

[1] Gwilt refers to Durand's *Précis des leçons d'architecture* (Paris, 1823).

[2] Lebrun, *Théorie de l'architecture grecque et romaine, déduite de l'analise des monumens antiques* (Paris, 1807).

[3] Gwilt's edition of Chambers's *Civil Architecture*, revised by W. H. Leeds in 1862, p. 118n.

[4] Cf. Percy E. Nobbs, *Design: a Treatise on the Discovery of Form*, p. 124, where the point is made that, far from expressing the laws of statics, Greek building practice never approached the structural limits of its materials.

[5] Article on proportion in Cresy's *Encyclopaedia of Civil Engineering*, incorporated in later editions of Gwilt's *Encyclopaedia of Architecture*, p. 900 in the edition of 1881.

[6] 9th edition, 1931, p. 336.   [7] See pp. 5–6 above.

was applied largely to the architecture of Greece. This was a natural thing to do, as the belief that Greek methods of design were based on arithmetic suggested an arithmetical approach to the problem of recovering these methods by analysis. The method has the very great advantage that the degree of approximation of ratios suggested by theory to measured ratios is immediately obvious. It can be stated in a quantitative form, as, for example, a percentage error. The method did not, however, reveal the presence in Greek architecture of the simply commensurable ratios which had been confidently expected, unless a fairly large margin of error was accepted.

The second method consists in the geometrical analysis of drawings prepared from measurements, and was applied to Gothic architecture and to a much smaller extent to Greek work. This again was a natural thing to do, since Gothic designers were obviously interested in geometry, and a geometrical method of analysis seemed at first sight most suitable. But unfortunately geometry is a much less reliable instrument of analysis than arithmetic. The excitement of discovering supposed coincidences in a drawing is not restrained by unsympathetic figures, and self-deception is easy.[1]

One of the great merits of Hambidge's contribution to the archaeology of proportion was to be that, although he believed Greek designs to have been carried out geometrically, he also saw that this was no obstacle to making use of the enormous advantages which arithmetic offered for analysis. It is for this reason that Hambidge's analyses are to be preferred to those of writers like Macody Lund and Moessel, however interesting their work may be in other respects.

Meanwhile in England the struggle of the minority of proportional theorists against the tendencies towards subjectivism seems almost to have died out in the second half of the nineteenth century, leaving architects disappointed in arithmetic and distrustful of geometry. Some gains had indeed been made in proportional theory, such as Lloyd's independent discovery of the principle of the repetition of ratios. The insistence on commensurable ratios was no longer felt to be indispensable, and root-rectangles had been brought into use by Kerrich and Hay. But the next important steps in the development of the theory of architectural proportion were to take place abroad.

---

[1] See L. D. Caskey's preface to Jay Hambidge's *The Parthenon and other Greek Temples: their Dynamic Symmetry* (1924), p. xiv, for a discussion of this point.

CHAPTER VI

THE RETURN TO
THE INCOMMENSURABLE (2)

GROWTH OF THE MODERN THEORY OF PROPORTION

(A) THE GOLDEN SECTION IN THE NINETEENTH CENTURY

The exact origin of the term 'golden section', 'section d'or', or 'goldener Schnitt' is far from certain, but Professor Archibald places it in Germany in the first half of the nineteenth century.[1] Apart from the obscurity in the name itself, it is also not very clear how far it is correct to speak of the rediscovery of the principle of the golden section in the nineteenth century. We have seen that the importance of the golden section in the Renaissance has been much exaggerated, and the evidence for its use in Greek design is entirely indirect. A fairly good case could be made out for the view that the nineteenth century actually discovered the golden section as an instrument of architectural proportion, however close earlier periods may have come to this discovery.

Michel objects to the statement that the golden section was rediscovered in the nineteenth century on different grounds, as he points out that in the form of the division of a line in 'extreme and mean ratio' it had been perfectly well known to the mathematicians of Western Europe since Campanus' Latin translation of Euclid from the Arabic in 1354.[2] He agrees, however, that interest in the golden section, apart from its mathematical role, was revived in the nineteenth century. As a matter of fact we shall see that mathematical interest in the golden section also came very much to life, although in quite a new form, in its connexion with the Fibonacci series, and indirectly in the properties of this series, which were studied from the point of view of the theory of numbers.

The first nineteenth-century writer on the application of the golden section to art seems to have been Zeising,[3] who 'tried to prove that the Golden Section is the key to all morphology, both in nature and art'.[4] Although Zeising's claims appear to

---

[1] In his contribution to Hambidge's *Dynamic Symmetry*, pp. 146 ff., based on an article in the *American Mathematical Monthly* (April–May 1918).　　[2] *De Pythagore à Euclide* (1950), pp. 600–1.

[3] E.g. in *Neue Lehre von den Proportionen des menschlichen Körpers* (Leipzig, 1854).

[4] Sir Herbert Read, *The Meaning of Art* (1931), p. 22 in the edition of 1949.

have been exaggerated and unscientific,[1] his work initiated a considerable literature on the subject in Germany, and was later rediscovered by Moessel, who based his own work on it. But what Danzig calls the 'modern revival of the golden section cult'[2] first came to the notice of the English-speaking world through the work on experimental aesthetics which was started by Fechner[3]. An account of his work was given, for instance, in 1892 by Bosanquet,[4] who himself uses the example of the golden section rectangle in discussing his own theory of the relationship of 'formal' beauty to 'concrete' beauty.[5] His account has been brought more up to date by Gilbert and Kuhn.[6]

Fechner, the founder of experimental aesthetics, carried out various experiments on the aesthetic preferences shown by people who were asked to choose between various simple forms. One of the things which he tried to find out was how far Zeising's claims on behalf of the golden section were justified. His experiments included the choice between various divisions of horizontal and vertical straight lines, of which one in each case was a golden section, and also the choice between various rectangles, of which one was a golden section rectangle. Bosanquet sums up the experiments on divisions of straight lines as follows: 'In dividing a horizontal line, the golden section is decidedly less pleasant than bisection. In dividing a vertical figure,...the golden section is less pleasant than the ratio 1:2.'[7]

The experiments on rectangles were more encouraging to supporters of the golden section. Ten rectangles were used of equal area, varying in shape from a square through a rectangle whose sides were in the ratio 21:34, and therefore very close to the ratio of the golden section, to a rectangle whose sides were in the ratio 2:5. Of these rectangles the most popular was the golden section rectangle, and the popularity of the others fell away towards the extremes, except that the square was rather more popular than its neighbour. A further important point is that, according to Bosanquet's account of the experiments, 'the simple rational relations (corresponding, it has been suggested, to musical consonance) show absolutely no superior pleasantness to those which can only be expressed by ratios of much larger numbers'.[8]

---

[1] See H. Osborne's *Theory of Beauty* (1952), p. 179.

[2] Tobias Danzig, *Number, the Language of Science* (1930). The discussion of the golden section occurs in an appendix called 'The Occult in Geometry', added to the second edition published in England in 1940. Danzig gives a short account of the 'geometrical occultism' of the ancients. He emphasizes the occult significance which they are supposed to have given to the golden section, but the only example which he gives of this is a quotation from Plato's *Timaeus* which seems to refer rather to geometrical proportion in general (p. 264). Of the 'modern revival of the golden section cult' he says (rather scornfully, one feels) that it is 'largely sponsored by artists', and goes on to point out the weaknesses of some attempted explanations of the value of the golden section.

[3] *Vorschule der Aesthetik* (1876).   [4] *History of Aesthetic* (1892), pp. 382–3.   [5] *Ibid.* pp. 40–1.

[6] *A History of Esthetics* (1939).   [7] *History of Aesthetic*, p. 383.   [8] *Ibid.*

But none of the rectangles provoked any very strong reactions, and 'the least deviation from symmetry has a far more decided unpleasantness than a proportionally much greater deviation from the golden section'.

These experiments have been much criticized and discussed. Various attempts have been made to explain them, and they have been repeated in different forms. Lightner Witmer, for instance, believed that Fechner had used too few rectangles, and that his experiments were not properly controlled. His own experiments seem to have suggested that the golden section possessed some value, both in the division of lines and in the formation of rectangles. Experiments were also carried out by R. P. Angier, but these seem to have had even less conclusive results.[1]

The series of experiments seems on the whole to have provided fairly faint praise for the golden section. Many explanations have been given for its supposed superiority, and are summarized by Gilbert and Kuhn.[2] A mathematical explanation assumes that the eye does in fact appreciate the repetition of ratios inherent in the golden section, which therefore gives us a measure of delight as an elementary example of unity and variety. This explanation was given by Wundt. The objection to it is, however, that the lengths whose ratios are equal are so arranged that the equality is not only not apparent to the eye, but is actually concealed from it. The explanation is in any case applicable only to divisions of lines, and not to the golden section rectangle.

A second, psychological explanation by Külpe, based on an application of Weber's law, seems to have been in effect very similar to the first. Another, physiological, explanation by Pierce is based on the movement of the eye muscles, and there has even been an attempt to explain the golden section in terms of psychoanalysis.[3]

The main objection to the whole theory is the fact that the results of the experiments are so very slight and inconclusive. The eye finds no real qualitative difference between the golden section and other ratios comparable, for instance, to the striking qualitative difference which the ear finds between consonance and dissonance in music. Gilbert and Kuhn sum up their discussion of the experiments by pointing out that 'the slightness of the emotional reaction gives rise to another objection. How can these hardly noticeable feelings contribute in any considerable degree to the exuberant delight often awakened by works of art?'[4]

Osborne makes the point that 'the aesthetic stimuli used in these experiments are so elementary…as to be sub-liminal for all, or all but an abnormally sensitive,

---

[1] D. Katz and H. S. Langfeld, article 'Aesthetics, Experimental', in the *Encyclopaedia Britannica* (1947).

[2] *A History of Esthetics*. The reader is referred to this work for a more detailed bibliography.

[3] A. Ehrenzweig, *The Psychoanalysis of Artistic Vision and Hearing* (1953), pp. 223–5.

[4] *A History of Esthetics*, p. 532.

aesthetic sense and it is probable that no purely aesthetic response could be obtained from them....There is inadequate complexity for perception in constructions of this kind.'[1] Osborne also quotes with approval Hambidge's remark that 'there is little ground for the assumption that any shape, *per se*, is more beautiful than any other'.[2]

The view which is put forward here is that the experiments failed to provide a convincing answer to the questions which they were intended to answer because they were based on a mistaken approach to the problem. It is probably true that the golden section has no aesthetic value in itself, but it is also true that it can be of value as a mathematical means to an aesthetic end. The experiments which were carried out were not framed to investigate this possibility, although there is no reason to suppose that experiments could not be designed for this purpose. The only positive result of the experiments has been, perhaps, to focus attention on the golden section, which had been little known before.

Meanwhile, while the psychologists had been carrying out these experiments, important developments had been going on in the field of mathematics. It was in the year 1876, when Fechner published his *Vorschule der Aesthetik*, that Lucas contributed a number of papers to French mathematical journals on the Fibonacci series and related topics.[3] The importance of the mathematical contribution was not so obvious at first sight, as it was expressed in terms of the theory of numbers rather than those of geometry, and the golden section only appeared indirectly through the relationship of its ratio to the Fibonacci series. But it is possible that in the long run the contribution of the mathematicians will have been more important than that of the psychologists.

Only a brief outline of this work can be given here, but detailed bibliographies are given by Professor Archibald,[4] and in Dickson's *History of the Theory of Numbers*.[5]

Already in 1732 Daniel Bernoulli had succeeded in expressing the general term of the Fibonacci series in terms of the number which we now call ϕ,[6] but this appears to have been overlooked, and it was not until 1843 that the result was rediscovered by Binet.[7] The work was taken up later by Lucas, who dealt with the

---

[1] *Theory of Beauty*, pp. 183–4.

[2] *Dynamic Symmetry*, p. 59. Nobbs, who described Hambidge as an 'architectural astrologer', is in complete agreement with him on this important point. Another critic of the aesthetic value of any particular shape or ratio is A. Trystan Edwards in *The Things which are Seen* (1921), p. 218 in the second edition of 1947, and *Style and Composition in Architecture* (1926), pp. 115 and 120–2 in the second edition of 1945.

[3] *Nouvelles correspondances mathématiques*, vol. II (1876), pp. 74–5 and 201–6, and *Comptes rendus de l'académie des sciences*, LXXXII (1876), pp. 165–7 and 1303–5.

[4] In Hambidge's *Dynamic Symmetry*, pp. 146 ff., and in the *American Mathematical Monthly* (April–May 1918).

[5] L. E. Dickson, *History of the Theory of Numbers*, vol. I (Carnegie Institute, 1919), ch. XVII.

[6] *Commentarii academiae scientiarum imperialis Petropolitanae*, vol. III (1732), p. 90.

[7] *Comptes rendus de l'académie des sciences*, XVII (1843), p. 563.

properties of two related series, which he called the u and v series. These were the Fibonacci series itself, 0, 1, 1, 2, 3, 5, 8, 13, 21, ..., and another series 2, 1, 3, 4, 7, 11, 18, 29, 47, ...

Lucas summarized his work in this field in an article in the *American Journal of Mathematics*,[1] in which he discussed the properties of three different types of series. One of these types is exemplified in the article by the Fibonacci series, related to the number ϕ, and also by what is called Pell's series, 0, 1, 2, 5, 12, 29, ..., which is related in precisely the same way to the number θ. It is this article which suggested to the present writer the possibility of using a proportional scale similar to Corbusier's Modulor, but based on the ratio $\theta : 1$ instead of the ratio $\phi : 1$. Other papers on the subject were written in the following years by d'Ocagne, Catalan, Liebetruth and Escott.

Before going on to discuss the application of the golden section in recent systems of proportion, we must first return to the vital principle of the repetition of similar figures, which was much clarified towards the end of the nineteenth century.

(B) THE PRINCIPLE OF THE REPETITION OF SIMILAR FIGURES

We have already seen how the principle of the repetition of ratios was stated independently by Barca in Italy and Lloyd in England. It would hardly be true to say that they discovered this principle of proportion, as we have found traces of its application in the work of Alberti and even Vitruvius, but they made explicit what before had been merely implied.

The approach by both Barca and Lloyd to the problem of proportion was analytical, and it was natural for them to express the principle in terms of the ratios of linear dimensions. Translated into the language of geometry, it becomes the principle of the repetition of similar figures. In this form it is even more obviously relevant to the problem of creating order of a kind apparent to the eye in works of architecture.

The principle was applied to the relationship of the parts of a design to the whole by Thiersch: 'We have found, in observing the most successful products of art in all important periods, that in each of them a fundamental shape is repeated, and that the parts form, by their composition and disposition, similar figures. Harmony results from the repetition of the fundamental form of the plan throughout its subdivisions.'[2]

---

[1] 'Théorie des fonctions numériques simplement périodiques', *American Journal of Mathematics*, 1 (1878), pp. 184 and 289 ff.

[2] The translation is from Professor Ghyka's article on Corbusier's Modulor in the *Architectural Review* (February 1948). The original is as follows: 'Wir finden, durch Betrachtung der gelungensten Werke aller Zeiten, dass in jedem Bauwerk eine Grundform sich wiederholt, dass die einzelnen Teile durch ihre Anordnung und Form stets einander ähnliche Figuren bilden. Das Harmonische entsteht durch Wiederholung der Hauptfigur des Werkes in seinen Unterabteilungen' (article on proportion in *Handbuch der Architektur*, vol. IV, Darmstadt, 1883, p. 39).

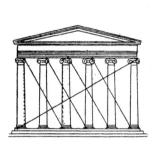

Abb. 3. Erechtheion
in Athen

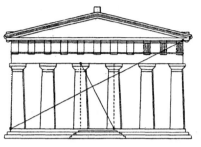

Abb. 1. Zeustempel
in Olympia

Abb. 4. Erechtheion
in Athen, Nordfront

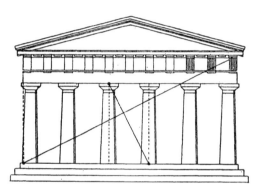

Abb. 2. Athene-Tempel auf Aegina

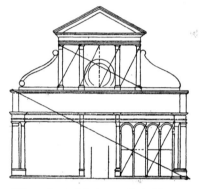

Abb. 5. Santa Maria novella in Florenz

Abb. 6. Cancelleria in Rom
Oberstes Flügelgeschoß

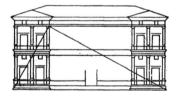

Abb. 7. Villa Farnesina in Rom

13. ANALYSES OF CLASSICAL BUILDINGS BY WÖLFFLIN

(From Heinrich Wölfflin's *Kleine Schriften*, 1946.)

Thiersch illustrated the principle by numerous analyses of the elevations of buildings. In these a dominant rectangle, often the whole facade, was indicated by one of its diagonals, and those parts which were of similar shape were shown in the same way.[1] In the stress on the rectangle and in the use of the diagonal in this way he was anticipating Hambidge.

Thiersch's theory had considerable influence. One of its enthusiastic supporters was Heinrich Wölfflin, who wrote an article on the subject in 1889, stressing in particular the importance of rectangles which were similar in shape but 'reversed in sense', or turned through a right angle. Wölfflin gave several analyses of classical buildings.[2] In some cases of reversed rectangles the smaller rectangle is what Hambidge was later to call the 'reciprocal' of the larger rectangle,[3] and sometimes the right angle between their diagonals occupied what Corbusier was to call 'the place of the right angle'.[4]

In the English-speaking world the principle of the repetition of similar figures first became well known through the work of the American John Beverly Robinson, published in 1899. Robinson spoke of the fundamental idea of proportion being that 'all the parts shall share the same general character—be what geometricians call "similar".... Used in this way architectural proportion becomes equivalent to arithmetical proportion [i.e. mathematical proportion] the dimensions of each part having the same ratio to each other as those of every other part.'[5] He qualified this, however, with a warning against cast-iron stiffness and lack of variety.

Like Thiersch and Wölfflin, Robinson used the diagonals of rectangles to indicate similar shapes in his analyses of classical buildings. He observed exceptions to the desirability of using similar figures, but concluded that 'the rule approaches the truth, the question only is as to the rule for divergencies from it; for which we are compelled, for the present, to trust to the vague faculty called taste'.[6]

The principle has been widely accepted since it was first stated. An exception is shown in the views of A. Trystan Edwards, who rejects it flatly: 'It has often been observed that the duplication in the same design of features of similar proportion, but of different sizes, is inadmissible. It is as if Nature, instead of making a baby of different proportions from those of an adult, had made him the exact replica of an adult, yet

---

[1] Thiersch's illustrations have often been reproduced, e.g. in Nobbs's *Design*, and in the article 'Proporzione—Architettura' in the *Enciclopedia Italiana* (Milan, 1936).

[2] *Zur Lehre von den Proportionen* (1889), reprinted in *Kleine Schriften* (Basle, 1946). See Plate 13.

[3] *Elements of Dynamic Symmetry*, p. 30.

[4] *The Modulor*, pp. 26–7 in the English edition of 1954.

[5] *Principles of Architectural Composition* (1899), p. 70.

[6] *Principles of Architectural Composition*, pp. 73–4.

cast in a smaller mould. Such a miniature man would be *out of scale* with his prototype.'[1]

Trystan Edwards's views deserve the most serious attention. In many respects his theories represent a return to the architectural principles of Alberti, expressed in a modern idiom. But in this case his rejection of similar shapes sounds like an arbitrary rule, which the argument from scale fails to support. The analogy with the human figure, which also reminds us of the Renaissance, is unsuccessful because the reason why a baby is a different shape from a man is what he would call 'subjectival', and not 'formal' at all. The baby is at an intermediate stage between a completely sessile and a completely mobile animal, and so its legs are shorter in proportion to its overall length than those of an adult. This sort of reason could not affect the purely formal relationships of rectangles.

As a matter of fact, the repetition of similar shapes can very well be considered as a method of fulfilling Trystan Edwards's own canon of 'Inflection', of which he says: '...Inflection was defined as a principle which secured the organic unity of an assemblage of objects by endowing them with a degree of sensibility manifested simultaneously in two ways: in the first place the objects must have a certain similarity, for otherwise we should be unable to recognise them as members of the same group; secondly, they must be suitably differentiated, for otherwise the parts would fail to express their natural differences in status, function, and position. Thus inflection can only be achieved by similarity associated with difference.'[2] The use of rectangles, similar in shape, but different in area, would seem to be one admirable way of satisfying these requirements.

The argument in favour of the repetition of similar shapes is put very well by Pearce: 'Consistent rectangles, or rectangles of similar proportions, have always been considered a unifying factor in composition, for we can, by this means, gain variety of area with unity of proportions.'[3] Nobbs, who agrees entirely with Trystan Edwards in ridiculing the aesthetic value of individual shapes and ratios, recognizes the value of the repetition of similar shapes: 'When consciously applied, as it no doubt has been by the recondite architects of sophisticated eras, recurring analogies of form at varied scales, but in constant proportion, afford a potent artifice for unification.'[4]

(C) RECENT SYSTEMS OF PROPORTION

In order to complete this historical account of the theory of proportion in architecture, it only remains for us to consider some of the more recent systems of

---

[1] *Style and Composition in Architecture*, pp. 128–9 in the second edition of 1944.
[2] *Style and Composition in Architecture*, 2nd ed. pp. 125–6.
[3] Cyril Pearce, *Composition* (1927), p. 54 in the 2nd edition of 1947. [4] *Design*, p. 145.

proportion. We shall start with purely geometrical systems, and show the transition through Hambidge's dynamic symmetry to the purely analytical system known as the Modulor.

(i) *Geometrical systems.* Macody Lund and Moessel relied, as we have noticed, on the geometrical method of analysing the proportions of ancient buildings. Macody Lund's work is best known to English readers, as an English translation of his *Ad Quadratum* exists.[1] Moessel's work is less familiar, though an account of it is given by Professor Ghyka.[2] Each of these writers attempted to reconstruct the methods of design used by Greek and Gothic architects.

Macody Lund's work was founded on that of earlier writers like Viollet-le-Duc, and he attached great importance to the use of the square and the equilateral triangle. He believed that the Greeks used expanding series of star-pentagons in their designs. These gave rise to the ϕ series, for which he substituted the Fibonacci series in his description. He traced the growing interest of later Gothic architects in the pentagon, and suggested that the golden section was being rediscovered by them, when their work was interrupted by the Black Death and what he believed was a 'decline of intellectualism' accompanying the Renaissance. Moessel's system also relied on polygons, with particular emphasis on the pentagon and the decagon. The stress is less upon expanding systems of star polygons than upon the use of controlling circles subdivided in various ways.

Although this type of 'circle geometry' was not regarded favourably by Hambidge himself,[3] Professor Ghyka considers that Moessel's use of it forms a satisfactory synthesis of the systems of Hambidge and Macody Lund: 'We see that Professor Moessel's solutions combine (without any previous knowledge of their theories) the starry diagrams of Lund with Hambidge's dynamic rectangles....'[4]

The general criticism of geometrical methods of analysis which we have already noted applies, however, as much to these systems as to their nineteenth-century predecessors. As attempts to analyse the proportions of buildings they lack the precision of arithmetical methods, and as attempts to reconstruct ancient systems of design they are inevitably highly speculative in the absence of direct literary evidence on the subject.

Quite apart from the archaeological interest of these systems, it is important to decide how far they are of practical value as systems of design for use today. Macody Lund, it is true, carried out his research into the methods of the past in order to assist in the practical task of restoring the cathedral of Nidaros. But if he

---

[1] F. Macody Lund, *Ad Quadratum* (1921).
[2] E.g. in *The Geometry of Art and Life*, pp. 140–3, and in *Geometrical Composition and Design*, pp. 42–8.
[3] *The Parthenon and other Greek Temples* (1924), p. 81.   [4] *The Geometry of Art and Life*, p. 143.

had been asked to invent a method suitable for designing a new cathedral, the result might have been quite different.

Professor Ghyka dismisses Macody Lund's work as consisting mostly of 'beautiful approximations'.[1] He tells us, however, that Moessel's system, like that of Hambidge, offers a useful technique of composition which is in fact in wide use.[2] In spite of this most architects will probably feel that Moessel's patterns of circles and polygons are as unsuitable for architectural design as Macody Lund's 'starry diagrams'.

The position is quite different in the case of Harry Roberts's geometrical system based on the use of various kinds of set-square. This system was designed primarily for ordinary day-to-day use in architectural practice. It is intended neither as a speculative reconstruction of a method used in the past, nor as a method of analysis of the work of the past, although it has been put to the latter use with interesting results.[3]

Roberts appears to have published no authoritative account of the use of his set-squares, although his book dealing with the ordinary $45°$ and $30°-60°$ set-squares is of the greatest interest.[4] The present short account of the system is based on a description given by his son,[5] and also on an article by Manning Robertson.[6]

R's set-squares can be regarded as an admirably quick method of drawing various types of rectangle which are of value in proportional schemes. Thus the quickest way of drawing a square is not with ruler and compass, but with a $45°$ set-square used to draw one of the diagonals. The value of a set-square is even clearer in the case of the $\sqrt{3}$ rectangle. Here the use of an ordinary scale to determine the lengths of the sides requires calculation, and the normal geometrical constructions are clumsy. But with the aid of a $30°-60°$ set-square the figure can be completed in a moment.

The fascinating things which can be done with the aid of the $45°$ and $30°-60°$ set-squares in the hands of a trained and skilful user are shown in Roberts's own book. Their use leads to the repetition of squares and $\sqrt{3}$ rectangles, and of rectangles related to them, and automatically produces a system of proportion similar to the one which Viollet-le-Duc attributed to the Gothic architects.[7] This system, however, appears on theoretical grounds to be of limited value. It did not satisfy Roberts, who designed a whole battery of special set-squares.

[1] *The Geometry of Art and Life*, p. 140.   [2] *Geometrical Composition and Design*, p. 47.
[3] E.g. by Manning Robertson in an article on 'The golden section or golden cut', published in the *R.I.B.A. Journal* (October, 1948).   [4] *R's Method of Using Ordinary Set Squares* (1927).
[5] A. Leonard Roberts, articles in *Architectural Design*, September 1948 to February 1949.
[6] *Loc. cit.*

[7] Its characteristic pattern of proportional relationships is the triple geometric progression based on the numbers $\sqrt{3}$, $1 + \sqrt{3}$ and 2.

R's set-squares produce a range of rectangles extending in a sort of octave from the square to the double square. Their ratios are as follows:

$$1:1 \quad 2\sqrt{2}:\sqrt{7} \quad 2:\sqrt{3} \quad 2:\phi \quad 4:3 \quad \sqrt{2}:1 \quad 3:2 \quad \phi:1 \quad \sqrt{3}:1 \quad \sqrt{7}:\sqrt{2} \quad 2:1$$

A detailed account of them is given by Leonard Roberts.[1] It is sufficient to point out here that, while some of these ratios like $\sqrt{3}:1$ and $\phi:1$ are unrelated and could not usefully be employed in the same design, the scale of rectangles can be divided into groups of rectangles which can be used together.

Thus Leonard Roberts explains the relationship to the golden section of the group of rectangles whose ratios are $1:1$, $2:\phi$, $\phi:1$ and $2:1$. If we include their reciprocals, we have a group of seven rectangles with the ratios $1:2$, $1:\phi$, $\phi:2$, $1:1$, $2:\phi$, $\phi:1$ and $2:1$.[2] In the same way we can choose four set-squares giving us a group of seven related rectangles with the simply commensurable ratios $1:2$, $2:3$, $3:4$, $1:1$, $4:3$, $3:2$ and $2:1$. It is obvious that we can choose further groups including rectangles with the ratios $\sqrt{2}:1$, $\sqrt{3}:1$ or $\sqrt{7}:\sqrt{2}$. The square and the double square are common to all these groups. With the exception of $\sqrt{7}:\sqrt{2}$ and $2\sqrt{2}:\sqrt{7}$, which were perhaps introduced to fill gaps in the scale, all the ratios concerned belong to familiar systems of proportion, and were evidently chosen to cover all systems of proportion which may reasonably be expected to be of use.

As a labour-saving device for drawing some of the most useful rectangles, R's set-squares cannot be excelled. The main criticism which can be made is that their effective use requires an enormous amount of knowledge and experience. In the first place, the complete range of set-squares supplies the key not to one, but to several systems of proportion, each of which would require considerable intellectual labour to master. In the second place, the method shares with other geometrical systems a major difficulty. This lies in the great complexity of the geometrical relationships of which a comprehensive knowledge is required. We shall shortly see how analytical systems relieve this complexity by reducing the problem from two dimensions to one.

On the other hand, the use of set-squares has the advantage that the repetition of similar figures, which we have decided to be the whole object of using a system of proportion, is much more under the designer's immediate control than is the case with an analytical system, where the result is achieved indirectly and figures in two dimensions are to some extent left to take care of themselves. Eventually it will perhaps become possible to define the fields in which geometrical systems, based on the use of set-squares on the one hand, and analytical systems, based on the use of scales on the other hand, are most useful.

[1] *Architectural Design* (October, 1948).   [2] *Ibid.* (February, 1949).

This account of geometrical systems of proportion would not be complete without some reference to the methods used by Sir Edwin Lutyens. An extremely interesting section on proportion occurs in the memoir by his son, who remarked that 'somebody will some day "discover" his system of applied geometry'.[1] Robert Lutyens elaborates the valuable idea of the 'armature of planes', a group of horizontal and vertical planes, of which the latter run in the directions of the main axes of the building. 'The "armature of planes", once conceived, cannot be overruled, but carries, in the multiplicity of its subdivisions, the occasion for any needed interval....The conception of a building must be of an integral composition whose unity is destroyed by additions, unless these additions are so designed that their "armature of planes" includes that of the existing building, and makes it part of a reintegrated whole.'[2]

Lutyens goes on to say that the vertical planes 'are usually equally spaced: that is, the horizontal intervals are in arithmetical progression, forming open sequences capable of extension. In a vertical direction, however, the major planes are usually at intervals in geometrical progression, forming a closed sequence.'[3] Here we are approaching an analytical rather than a geometrical system. It is, however, important to point out that there are serious objections to the use of the arithmetical progression horizontally and the geometrical progression vertically. The method, by restricting proportion to one dimension only, destroys its power of facilitating the repetition of similar figures in two dimensions.

This confusion of the distinction between symmetry and proportion with the distinction between horizontal and vertical articulation in architecture goes back to Ruskin.[4] It is based on the perfectly correct observation that bilateral symmetry is not desirable for vertical divisions, since it does not reflect the important difference between the top and the bottom of a building. However, the argument against using bilateral or even repeat symmetry for vertical divisions cannot be an argument against using proportion for horizontal divisions.

But it is not quite clear how far the 'armature of planes' represents Sir Edwin Lutyens's ideas, and how far it is a development of those ideas by his son. Robert Lutyens himself explains that he is interpreting his father's ideas fairly freely, and Hussey in his biography denies that Lutyens practised an elaborate and preconceived system of proportion at all. His 'office ratios' were developed by trial and error.[5]

---

[1] Robert Lutyens, *Sir Edwin Lutyens: an Appreciation in Perspective* (1942), p. 15.

[2] *Ibid.* pp. 59–60. [3] *Ibid.* p. 60.

[4] In *The Seven Lamps of Architecture* (1907 edition), p. 130, Ruskin speaks of 'the connection of Symmetry with horizontal and Proportion with vertical division. Evidently there is in symmetry a sense not merely of equality, but of balance: now a thing cannot be balanced by another on top of it, though it may by one at the side of it.' He goes on to extend this argument to repeat symmetry, but here his reasoning is less convincing. [5] Christopher Hussey, *The Life of Sir Edwin Lutyens* (1950), p. 164.

But both writers make it clear that Sir Edwin Lutyens did in fact practice the repetition of similar figures. In his earlier work he used the ϕ rectangle, as at Hampstead Garden City Institute, and later he changed over to the $\sqrt{2}$ rectangle, as at Gledstone.[1] In what Hussey calls his 'Elemental Mode' he used ratios chosen to suit the work in hand, like the ratio of $2\frac{1}{2}:1$ used for the arched openings of the Thiepval Memorial, or the ratio of $3:1$ used for the cathedral at Liverpool.[2]

The transition from the ϕ rectangle to the $\sqrt{2}$ rectangle might appear to be a retrogressive step to those who see no virtue in any system of proportion not based on the golden section. But although $\sqrt{2}$ and the associated number θ have certain limitations compared to ϕ, they also have great advantages, provided that the limitations can be overcome. They have a far richer geometrical background, being related to the radial symmetry of the square, the octagon, and various star octagons, to the proportions of expanding systems of squares and circles and of star octagons, and to systems of repeat symmetry based on the square. An example of the value of $\sqrt{2}$ is shown in the way in which Robert Lutyens is able to turn his armature of planes through $45°$ to produce a secondary armature. Against all this the golden section can show only the pentagon and the decagon, neither of them very useful figures in architecture.

It is therefore just possible that Sir Edwin Lutyens's change from ϕ to $\sqrt{2}$ will turn out to have been, not retrogressive, but an experiment of the greatest value.

(ii) *Introduction to analytical systems of proportion.* The great analytical systems of the past, those of the Renaissance, were based on the simple arithmetic of commensurable ratios. At that time the arithmetical technique for dealing with incommensurable ratios was not sufficiently well known to be used freely. Systems of proportion employing incommensurable ratios like $\sqrt{2}:1$ or $\sqrt{3}:1$ have normally been based on geometrical methods.

What is new about the more recent systems developed by Hambidge and Corbusier is that they successfuly combine the advantages of analytical systems with the use of incommensurable ratios. Hambidge's system shows some features of a transitional stage of development from the geometrical to the analytical. His analytical system is based on the manipulation of incommensurable ratios expressed in ordinary decimal notation, and although well within the mathematical powers of the average architect, it is in practice somewhat clumsy. Corbusier has developed an analytical system which does away with the need for any calculations, at the cost of restricting the user to a fixed scale of dimensions, which, when used consistently, seems to give a much less flexible system than Hambidge's.

[1] *Sir Edwin Lutyens: an Appreciation in Perspective*, p. 64.
[2] *The Life of Sir Edwin Lutyens*, pp. 475 and 531 ff.

Analytical systems are those in which the problem of proportion is reduced from two or three dimensions to one. The manipulation of geometrical shapes is replaced by the manipulation of linear dimensions. The repetition of similar shapes, the end in view, recedes into the background, and attention is directed to the means to that end, the proportional relationships between linear dimensions.

But at the cost of this loss of directness of method, analytical systems have an enormous advantage over geometrical systems. This arises from the fact that the additive properties of geometrical figures, by means of which smaller parts are built up into larger parts and larger parts into wholes, are extremely complicated. The reduction of the number of dimensions from two to one very greatly reduces the number of additive properties with which the designer is concerned, and it becomes a comparatively simple matter to learn them. Hambidge himself justifies his use of arithmetic as a labour-saving device: 'If we followed the steps of the Greeks and acquired our knowledge of these shapes entirely by geometrical construction, the labour would be too great for an ordinary lifetime.'[1] The reason for using incommensurable rather than commensurable ratios is of course the increased flexibility due to the numerous additive properties of geometric progressions based on ϕ and θ, compared with those based on whole numbers.

Before we examine Hambidge's 'dynamic symmetry' and Corbusier's 'Modulor' in slightly more detail, something must be said about the very important contribution of William Schooling. Schooling's work is incorporated in one of Sir Theodore Cook's books on spiral forms.[2] The most important of the spirals occurring in nature which are discussed in this book is the geometric spiral, and the study of geometric spirals leads to the study of the geometric progressions associated with them. Of these the one which most interested Sir Theodore Cook was the ϕ series, and it is with this that Schooling's work is concerned.

The great importance of Schooling's contribution lies in the fact that he turns our attention from the golden section considered as an isolated geometric construction to the geometric progression based on the number ϕ. The importance of the geometric progression in proportion is taken for granted. He does, however, state the property of the ϕ series which gives it its peculiar value. It 'is the only geometric progression the successive terms of which can be obtained by addition as well as by multiplication by the common ratio in the ordinary way'. While it was not perhaps the first time that the value of the geometric progression had been consciously realized, it was the first time that the importance of the additive properties of a geometric progression had been stressed.

In addition to this Schooling stated many of the other mathematical properties of

[1] *Dynamic Symmetry*, p. 73.   [2] *The Curves of Life*, 1914.

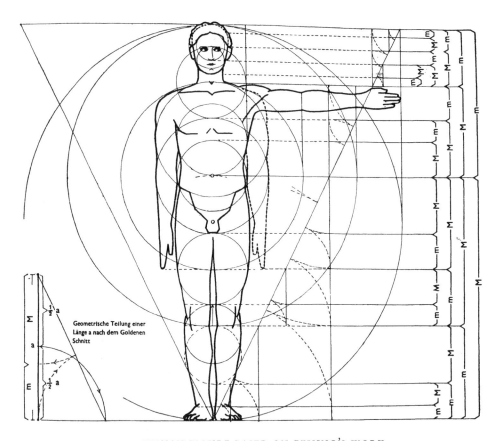

Geometrische Teilung einer
Länge a nach dem Goldenen
Schnitt

14. HUMAN FIGURE BASED ON ZEISING'S WORK

Analysis by means of golden sections conceals the ϕ series. (From Professor Ernst
Neufert's *Bauentwurfslehre*.)

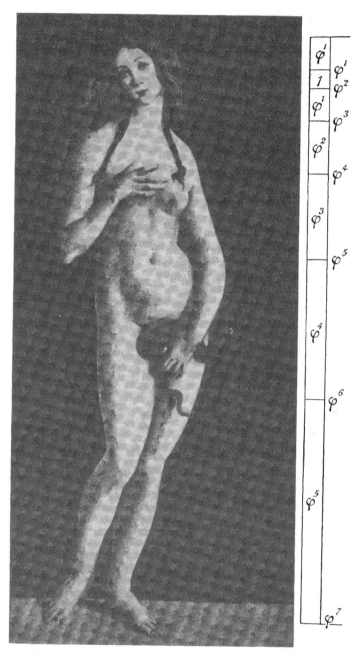

15. SIR THEODORE COOK'S ANALYSIS OF A BOTTICELLI VENUS

The use of the ϕ series. (From *The Curves of Life*, pl. viii, 'Venus, by Sandro Botticelli'.)

the ϕ series, and its relationship to the Fibonacci series. It was he who introduced the simple but extremely valuable device of using the symbol ϕ, invented for the purpose by Mark Barr, to describe the ratio of the golden section.[1] The great value of this simple innovation in theoretical analysis is shown, for instance, in comparing the human figure based on Zeising's work, from Professor Neufert's *Bauentwurfslehre*, with Sir Theodore Cook's analysis of the Botticelli Venus.[2] Both depend on golden sections, and in the first drawing each separate golden section has the major and minor parts indicated by the letters *M* and *m*. To trace the relationship of dimensions which are not immediately connected by a golden section is a lengthy operation. In the second example, although the analysis is not carried so far, each dimension is expressed as a power of ϕ. It is therefore possible not only to pick out the golden sections, but to compare any of the dimensions in the analysis at a glance.

We shall shortly have to consider how it is that Hambidge used no method of this sort in his own work, and, although he was well aware of the importance of the ϕ series, preferred to rely on the notation of ordinary arithmetic to describe it. Meanwhile it is interesting to notice that of several writers who today use the symbol ϕ, few do so in the way in which Schooling intended, or obtain the full benefit from his notation. It is quite common to use ϕ purely as a sort of literary shorthand for 'golden section', so that the golden section ratio becomes the ϕ ratio, the golden section rectangle becomes the ϕ rectangle, and so forth. While this is perfectly justified, the symbol ϕ was not intended merely for use in this way, but primarily as a mathematical symbol. Those writers who explain to us that ϕ is equal to 1·618, but relapse into decimal notation when it becomes necessary to manipulate this number and its powers, or to analyse the proportions of a drawing, are losing much of the value of Schooling's invention.

Apart from Schooling's theoretical contribution, *The Curves of Life* contains a technical device of great interest.[3] This is a 'universal ϕ scale', which consists of two parallel lines, each divided in the same way in a series of golden sections like the 'red' or 'blue' scales of Corbusier's Modulor. Between these parallel lines or scales run a series of diagonal lines connecting each division of the lower scale to the next division of the upper scale. The value of the device is that any line drawn parallel to the two scales is itself divided up by the diagonal lines into divisions which form a ϕ scale. It therefore provides a means of constructing a ϕ scale ascending and descending from any dimension we like to choose.

---

[1] Other symbols for ϕ or its reciprocal have been used, e.g. by Sir D'Arcy Wentworth Thompson in an article in *Mind*, xxxviii, 1929, and by Danzig in *Number, the Language of Science* (2nd English edition, 1940).

[2] See Plates 14 and 15.   [3] See Plate 16.

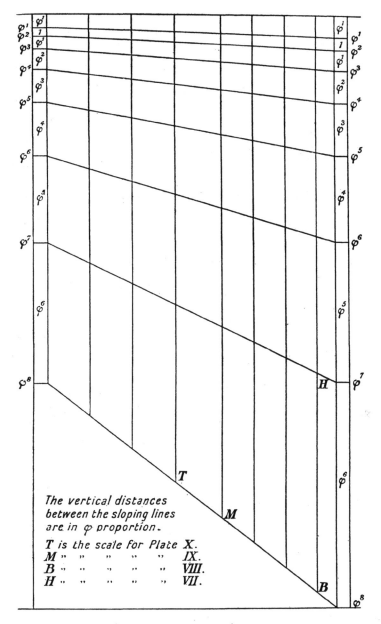

The vertical distances
between the sloping lines
are in φ proportion.

T is the scale for Plate X.
M " " " " IX.
B " " " " VIII.
H " " " " VII.

16. THE UNIVERSAL φ SCALE

A forerunner of the Modulor. (From Cook's *Curves of Life*, pl. ix, 'A scale of phi proportions'.)

Sir Theodore Cook's readers were invited to use it for anlysing the proportions of paintings, selecting a scale to fit the work under consideration. Its value as an instrument of design is also obvious, as the user has at his disposal not merely one scale, but a scale which can be varied to suit the requirements of his programme.

This anticipation of the principle of the Modulor aroused far less interest than it deserved in the country of its origin, perhaps because of the unfortunate date of its publication. Occasional references to the work of Schooling and Sir Theodore Cook occurred between the wars,[1] but it must be admitted that its value was recognized more clearly abroad. The growth of interest in it in England is partly due to the influence of writers like Professor Ghyka.

(iii) *Dynamic symmetry*. A detailed account of Hambidge's work is impossible here, and for this the reader must be referred to Hambidge's own writings,[2] and to those of Caskey.[3] Professor Ghyka attaches the greatest importance to Hambidge's ideas,[4] and a particularly clear account of his main principles, illustrated by his analysis of the Parthenon, is given by Walter Dorwin Teague.[5]

Hambidge's work has two aspects, the analysis of works of the past, and the elaboration of a system of design for use today. He himself stresses the difference, pointing out that while the work of analysis is inevitably intricate and tedious, a system of design must be simple to use. Amongst general principles of proportion, Hambidge recognizes the importance of the repetition of similar shapes: 'Symmetry [by which he means proportion] is immediately connected with design, and design depends to a great extent on similarity of figure....'[6] The importance of similar figures in practice is obvious throughout his work. Like Thiersch and Robinson he uses diagonals to define rectangles and indicate their similarity of shape.

Hambidge also attaches the greatest importance to the geometric progression, particularly the ϕ series, which he describes in decimal notation. His interest in it appears to have been aroused in the first place, like that of Sir Theodore Cook, by the study of logarithmic spirals. Although Hambidge never introduces his readers openly to the θ series, a careful search will reveal it in his work, playing the same part in relation to $\sqrt{2}$ that the ϕ series plays in relation to $\sqrt{5}$.

But before the different types of dynamic symmetry are discussed in detail, something must be said about the important and rather intricate distinction between dynamic symmetry and static symmetry. At times this distinction seems to approach

[1] E.g. in R. A. Duncan's *Architecture of a New Era* (1933), p. 125.
[2] E.g. *Dynamic Symmetry, The Parthenon and other Greek Temples*, and *The Elements of Dynamic Symmetry*.
[3] *Geometry of Greek Vases* (1922).
[4] *The Geometry of Art and Life*, and *Geometrical Composition and Design*.
[5] *Design This Day*.   [6] *Elements of Dynamic Symmetry*, p. 101.

fairly closely to the distinction which has been made here between proportion in the narrower sense and symmetry, especially radial symmetry. Thus, static symmetry is 'apparent in nature in certain crystal forms, radiolaria, diatoms, flowers, and seed pods, and has been used consciously in art at several periods. The principle of dynamic symmetry is manifest in shell growth and in leaf distribution in plants. A study of the basis of design in art shows that this active symmetry was known to but two peoples, the Egyptians and the Greeks.'[1] Again, 'Static Symmetry, as found in both nature and art, often, is radial. In this respect it is a symmetry of focus, an orderly distribution of shapes or composing units of form about a center. Almost invariably these units of form are parts or logical subdivisions of the regular figures, the equilateral triangle, the square and the regular pentagon.'[2] But it turns out that static symmetry also includes genuine systems of proportion based on *expanding* systems of squares or triangles, and on the use of commensurable ratios.

At other times, especially in Hambidge's analysis of Greek work, a different aspect of the distinction between static and dynamic symmetry is stressed. This distinction is identical with the one which we have made between the comparatively inflexible systems of proportion based on the use of commensurable ratios, and the comparatively flexible systems based on the use of incommensurable ratios like $\phi : 1$ and $\theta : 1$. 'Greek practice in static symmetry was not essentially different from what it was in dynamic. The latter type was simply a more powerful and flexible instrument.'[3] But the $\sqrt{2}$ and $\sqrt{3}$ rectangles also occur in static symmetry, 'produced as logical divisions of some regular figure'.[4]

The true nature of the distinction seems to be that Hambidge regarded as an example of dynamic symmetry any genuine system of proportion based on the use of incommensurable ratios, but excluded systems based on the rigid radial symmetry of expanding systems of geometrical figures. These were classed as static symmetry, along with everything else from genuine systems of proportion based on commensurable ratios to systems of symmetry using regular geometrical figures. For Hambidge the peculiar quality of vitality of dynamic symmetry lay in its freedom from the set patterns of symmetry in the normal sense of the word, together with its superior flexibility compared with systems of proportion based on the use of commensurable ratios.

The flexibility of systems of proportion based on numbers like ϕ and θ is derived from the variety of additive properties of certain geometric progressions like the ϕ and θ series. This fact is not brought out at all clearly either by geometry or by arithmetic, but only by Schooling's analytical technique, so perhaps Hambidge was not clearly conscious of it.

[1] *Dynamic Symmetry*, p. 7. [2] *Ibid.* p. 138.
[3] *Ibid.* pp. 141–2. [4] *Ibid.* p. 140.

He himself attached a great deal of importance to the fact that the root-rectangles, which from a geometrical point of view play an important part in dynamic symmetry, have sides which are commensurable, not in length, but in the areas of the squares upon them. Vitruvius' insistence on commensurability in length was a distorted echo of the Greek theory, which had been based on commensurability of area.

Now whether this historical theory is true or not, the actual importance of this property of commensurability in square in Hambidge's own system can be greatly exaggerated. The majority of rectangles which he uses are not the root-rectangles themselves, but rectangles derived from them whose sides are commensurable neither in length nor in square.

It is perfectly true that Greek mathematicians were interested in commensurability in square. Hambidge was very much astonished to discover that the Greek term δυνάμει σύμμετρος, which Euclid uses in the sense 'commensurable in square', was so similar to the term 'dynamic symmetry', which he had coined quite independently to describe the system of proportion which he attributed to the Greeks.[1]

Hambidge's reconstruction of what he believed to be the Greek system of proportion is based mainly on the analysis of vases. This had the advantage that there were a large number of examples readily available in the museums. They were usually in good condition, and could be measured quickly and accurately. The cumulative effect of the large number of analyses by both Hambidge and Caskey is even more impressive than Hambidge's work on a comparatively small number of Greek buildings.

A limited number of the vases which were analysed were found to be based on a type of static symmetry, consisting in the use of simply commensurable ratios. But the great majority could only be analysed in terms of dynamic symmetry. Of these a small number were based on ratios related to $\sqrt{3}$, rather more on ratios related to $\sqrt{2}$ and the θ series, and the great majority on $\sqrt{5}$ and the ϕ series. Caskey gives a table showing the results for 185 vases. Of these, 3 could not be analysed, 18 were examples of static symmetry, and the remaining 164 were examples of dynamic symmetry. Of the latter, 6 were based on $\sqrt{3}$, 22 on $\sqrt{2}$ and θ, and the remaining 136 on $\sqrt{5}$ and ϕ.[2] If these results are accepted, it seems to suggest that the Greeks found out in practice that the rich variety of additive properties of the ϕ series gives great flexibility to systems of proportion based upon it.

Hambidge believed that he could trace a historical sequence in the use of these

---

[1] *The Parthenon and other Greek Temples*, p. 1, and *Elements of Dynamic Symmetry*, p. 129. The Greek term occurs, for instance, in Euclid's 'Elements', book x, defn. 2.

[2] *Geometry of Greek Vases*, p. 25.

different systems. Static symmetry was used in the earliest period, and gave way to dynamic symmetry based sometimes on $\sqrt{2}$ or $\sqrt{3}$ rectangles, but mainly in the classical period on $\sqrt{5}$ rectangles. In the Greco-Roman period dynamic symmetry faded out. In Hambidge's own words, 'this loss was a calamity. We must either blame the Romans for this catastrophe, or ascribe it to a general deterioration of intelligence'.[1]

But the disappearance of dynamic symmetry, at least in architecture, might also be explained by the fact that it was an elaborate form of applied mathematics. While Athens might be able to train designers for its use on a comparatively small scale, it had to be replaced by simpler though clumsier methods of solving the more complicated and more numerous problems set by the expanding needs of the later period.

The methods of design which Hambidge believed the Greeks themselves to have used are geometrical. The possible relationship which he indicated between proportional design and mathematical theory is of the highest interest. Pennethorne had already suggested that it was art which provided the stimulus to mathematical studies in Greece,[2] and Cantor believed that there was a connexion between the appearance of the golden section in Greek architecture and developments in Greek mathematics.[3] But Hambidge went much further in tracing a detailed connexion between Greek art and Greek mathematics.

We have already seen that the geometrical technique which he attributed to the Greeks included the use of root-rectangles and the manipulation of similar figures, especially the 'reciprocals' of rectangles, by means of the diagonal. Of the greatest importance from the point of view of the history of Greek mathematics is his reference to 'the application of areas': 'For the purpose of dividing up the areas of rectangles so that the divisions would be recognizable, the Greeks had recourse to a simple but ingenious method which is called "the application of areas". This idea was used by them both in science and in art.'[4] He goes on to show how the application of a square to the end of a ϕ rectangle, and inside it, leaves its reciprocal, a smaller ϕ rectangle. In the same way the application of a square inside the end of a $\sqrt{2}$ rectangle leaves a θ rectangle, and the application of a square inside the end of a θ rectangle leaves a $\sqrt{2}$ rectangle.

[1] *Dynamic Symmetry*, p. 157.   [2] *Elements and Mathematical Principles*, p. 9.

[3] 'Der goldne Schnitt spielte in der griechischen Baukunst der perikleischen Zeit eine nicht zu verkennende Rolle. Das ästhetisch wirksamste Verhältniss, und das ist das stetige, ist in den athenischen Bauten aus den Jahren 450–430 aufs schönste verwerthet. Wir können bei solcher Regelmässigkeit des Auftretens nicht an ein instinktives Zutreffen glauben, am wenigsten, wenn wir des eben berührten geistigen Zusammenhangs zwischen goldnem Schnitte, regelmässigem Fünfecke und pythagoräischem Lehrsatze gedenken'; Cantor, *Vorlesungen über Geschichte der Mathematik* (2nd edition), vol. I, pp. 166–7, quoted by Macody Lund in *Ad Quadratum*, vol. I, p. 139n.   [4] *Elements of Dynamic Symmetry*, p. 28.

There is no need to enter into these geometrical operations in any further detail here. But it is worth noting that the 'application of areas' is one of what Heath describes as the two 'great engines of Greek geometrical algebra'.[1] The other was the method of proportions, but before the time of Eudoxus this was restricted to handling commensurable ratios only. It could not, therefore, have been connected with the development of dynamic symmetry, and its discovery is usually believed to have been associated with the study of musical intervals by the Pythagoreans. There is thus a fascinating possibility that of these two great intellectual tools, the invention of one, the application of areas, was stimulated by the growth of the visual arts, while the invention of the other, the numerical theory of proportion, was stimulated by the growth of music.

We come finally to the methods which Hambidge suggested for the use of present-day designers. As we have seen, he felt that the use of arithmetic provided a short cut to a knowledge of the mathematical relationships arising out of Greek geometry. But for the actual operation of drawing the rectangles of dynamic symmetry, his students were advised to practise both geometrical and arithmetical methods. The arithmetical method required the use of a 'scale divided into millimetres, or a foot-rule divided into tenths'.[2] Unfortunately, it also required rather intricate arithmetical calculations. It is for this reason that Walter Dorwin Teague rejects Hambidge's arithmetic in favour of a return to a simpler form of geometry.[3]

There is, however, a means of avoiding the difficulties both of geometry and of arithmetic, although it may lead to some loss of flexibility. This is the completely analytical method, based on the use of scales like Corbusier's Modulor, which can be manipulated by means of rules for which calculation is not required at all.

For the purpose of theoretical analysis, on the other hand, the disadvantages of Hambidge's arithmetic can be avoided to a great extent by Schooling's technique of using mathematical symbols like ϕ to replace the clumsiness of the usual arithmetical notation. It is not very clear, for instance, that a rectangle whose sides are 0·691 and 0·309 is a $\sqrt{5}$ rectangle.[4] But if these numbers are replaced by the symbols $\sqrt{5}/2\phi$ and $1/2\phi$, the fact is obvious at a glance. Hambidge himself explains why he rejects the use of symbols of this type: '...symmetry is immediately connected with design and design depends to a great extent on similarity of figure....If we used algebraic symbols for the units of dynamic symmetry we should have too great a confusion of values within a specific design example. Moreover the average designer or the average layman is not sufficiently familiar with the processes of either algebra or geometry....'[5]

[1] *Greek Mathematics*, vol. i, pp. 150–4. [2] *Elements of Dynamic Symmetry*, p. 118.
[3] *Design This Day*, p. 128. [4] *Elements of Dynamic Symmetry*, p. 99, fig. 104. [5] *Ibid.* p. 101.

But the example we have just given shows how the use of symbols often makes ratios much easier to recognize than the use of arithmetic. Easy identification of ratios leads to easy recognition of similar figures. Nearly all the dimensions in the examples in *Elements of Dynamic Symmetry*, for instance, can be expressed very simply in terms of ϕ and $\sqrt{5}$ or θ and $\sqrt{2}$. In these cases the proportional relationships between them are made immediately obvious. But in the analyses of actual Greek work in *Dynamic Symmetry* itself this becomes much more difficult. If Hambidge's analyses are accepted, it looks as though the Greeks did not restrict themselves to the use of the simpler geometric progressions associated with ϕ and θ. Using the method of geometry, there is no reason why they should have done so, and this is the real justification for Hambidge's rejection of symbols.

The complexity of Hambidge's arithmetic is due to the fact that his methods were first invented for the purpose of archaeological research. As he himself realized, the problem of practical design is a very different one. For this purpose we can either go back to geometry, as Walter Dorwin Teague suggests, or forward to a fully analytical method.

(iv) *The Modulor*. Finally, we come to the main example of an entirely analytical method of proportion, the use of Corbusier's Modulor. This method dispenses wholly with calculation, so to call it 'analytical' may seem misleading. It is, however, analytical in the sense that the problem of proportion is reduced from two or three dimensions to one, whereas dynamic symmetry retains a geometrical element.

Some short accounts of the Modulor include an explanation of it by Professor Ghyka,[1] and a lecture on the subject by Corbusier himself.[2] The main account is provided of course by Corbusier's book, which has now been translated into English.[3]

The Modulor consists of two scales, the 'red' scale and the 'blue' scale. The dimensions of the 'blue' scale are double those of the 'red', and the divisions of each scale are based on the ϕ series. They form the following pattern:

Some illustrations which have appeared of the Modulor show a series of sub-divisions. No explanation of these subdivisions has been given, and they are omitted from Corbusier's book, although they are occasionally used in examples of designs based on the Modulor which he gives. They are obviously formed by adding the

[1] *Architectural Review* (February, 1948).

[2] Lecture to students at the Architectural Association School, reported in the *Architects' Journal*, 8 January 1948.

[3] *The Modulor*, translated by Peter de Francia and Anna Bostock, 1954.

dimensions of each scale together in pairs. The addition of these subdivisions to the Modulor increases very greatly the additive properties of its dimensions, and therefore its flexibility. But it also increases the number of shapes which the scale will produce, so that their indiscriminate use would tend to destroy its effectiveness as a system of proportion.

If we ignore these subdivisions, we are left with a Modulor consisting of the red and blue ϕ scales, the dimensions of the second being double those of the first. The addition of the second scale greatly increases the flexibility of the Modulor. It places at the user's disposal additional additive properties such as $2\phi^2 = 1 + \phi^3$, as well as the almost indispensable additive property $2 = 1 + 1$. In spite of this the Modulor without its subdivisions still has a rather limited range of additive properties. We shall return to this fact shortly, as it seems to be reflected in the way in which the scale has been used.

In addition to the proportional properties of the scale, we have also to consider the actual values of the dimensions themselves. It is important to realize that the Modulor is not only an instrument of architectural proportion, a means of ensuring the repetition of similar shapes. It is also a system of preferred dimensions intended for standardizing the sizes of mass-produced building components. Most systems of this type which have been developed entirely ignore the problem of architectural proportion. It has been assumed that this problem could safely be left to the architect.[1] But as Dr Martin has pointed out,[2] by the time the dimensions have been fixed it may well be too late for the architect to introduce proportion into his design. The Modulor provides dimensions which not only allow him to do so, but do it for him almost automatically.

Two features of the scale are of the greatest interest, and are stressed by Corbusier himself. The first of these is the relationship of the scale to the human figure. The claim has often been made for systems of proportion in the past that they are based on the proportions of the human body, but we have not been inclined to take these claims very seriously. What is much more important about the Modulor is the fact that it includes a number of dimensions taken from the body of a 6-foot man in various positions. Corbusier can therefore reasonably make the claim that it is more suitable for designing articles of furniture and other 'extensions' of the human figure than a scale derived from some arbitrary unit like the 4 in. module or the metre.

The second feature of interest is the way in which the scale is intended to bridge

[1] The work of the Building Research Station forms an important exception. See a paper presented to the Modular Society by W. A. Allen on 'Modular co-ordination research: the evolving pattern' (*R.I.B.A. Journal*, April, 1955).

[2] Dr J. L. Martin's broadcast talk on 'Building, measure and man', B.B.C. Third Programme, 22 November 1954.

the gulf between the world of metres and centimetres and the world of feet and inches. In its original form the red scale contained the dimension 175·0 cm., representing the height of a man. Fixing one dimension in this way fixed all the others. The next step downwards on the red scale gave a dimension of 108·2 cm., which was supposed to represent the height of the man's navel. Doubling this dimension gave 216·4 cm. on the blue scale, the height of a man with his arm raised.

These dimensions were, however, extremely clumsy when they were translated into feet and inches. Corbusier describes the surprising effect of making the height of the man equal to 6 feet instead of 175 cm.: 'To our delight, the graduations of a new "Modulor", based on a man 6 feet tall, translated themselves before our eyes into round figures in feet and inches!'[1]

The dimensions of the new Modulor can in fact be expressed fairly accurately in terms of half-inches. This is because the dimension which determines all the others, 6 feet, is equal to 144 half-inches, and 144 is a number of the Fibonacci series; so the red scale can be obtained from the Fibonacci series by using a half-inch module, and the blue scale can be obtained in the same way by using an inch module:

Red   4 in. $6\frac{1}{2}$ in. $10\frac{1}{2}$ in.   17 in. $27\frac{1}{2}$ in. $44\frac{1}{2}$ in.   72 in. $116\frac{1}{2}$ in. ...

Blue   8 in.   13 in.   21 in.   34 in.   55 in.   89 in.   144 in.   233 in. ...

Corbusier also gives the scales based on the ϕ series itself, expressing the dimensions to three places of decimals, but the simpler working dimensions, or 'valeurs d'usage', provide a satisfactory approximation.

Not only was the original Modulor altered to fit the 6-foot Englishman, but Corbusier is even prepared on occasion to design a special Modulor to suit a special job.[2] This possibility of designing scales for special occasions, or a series of alternative scales, is of the greatest interest. It would be of value, for instance, for buildings on restricted sites, or where for some other reason the programme contains dimensions which are more or less fixed.

Corbusier has told us the story of the origin of the Modulor in detail. It is important to notice here that the original conception was not one of a continuous linear scale, stretching downwards and upwards as far as required, but of a grid of proportions limited to a few dimensions only. This grid was to be a two-dimensional affair, incorporating three features to which Corbusier attached particular importance. These were the height of the man with his arm raised, and two geometrical constructions which had been found useful in proportion, the golden section and what Corbusier calls 'the place of the right angle'. This is the method of drawing a rectangle and its reciprocal with their diagonals at right angles to each other, and it automatically generates the first three terms of a geometric progression.

[1] *The Modulor*, p. 56.   [2] *Ibid.* p. 163.

In the original problem set by Corbusier,[1] that of a square riding on a double-square, the right angle was given an impossible task. The problem itself was therefore insoluble, but the attempt at solving it produced 'an efflorescence of golden sections',[2] and led almost accidentally to the invention of the Modulor. This linear scale was very unlike the two-dimensional grid which he had set out to discover.

Corbusier's account of this curious origin of the Modulor shows that its discovery was quite independent of Schooling's work on the ϕ series. Corbusier does, it is true, use the symbol ϕ from time to time. He uses it, however, purely in what we have described as 'literary' shorthand in such phrases as 'rapport ϕ' and 'série ϕ'. It seems fairly obvious that he had no first-hand knowledge of Schooling's work, and that this deprived him of a valuable short-cut towards the discovery of the Modulor.

What is perhaps more important is the fact that although the limited proportional grid gave way to a linear scale extending indefinitely, traces of it still seem to play a part in the theory and practice of the Modulor. It seems to survive in the idea of the 'textural unity' which the Modulor produces in the 'unité d'habitation' at Marseilles: '...the systematic application of the harmonious measures of the "Modulor" create a unitary *state of aggregation* that may be described as "textural".'[3]

The description of the building shows how the Modulor was used for determining the dimensions of a great variety of detail. But although the additive properties of the scale are used to some extent the process is never carried very far. The Modulor provided the dimensions of the individual flats, of various structures on the roof, and of some decorative sculpture, but not, apparently, the larger dimensions of the building. The number of dimensions which are used are, indeed, claimed to amount to only fifteen. These are incorporated in the 'stele of the measure',[4] and cover only a very limited range of the dimensions of the Modulor. They extend from 6·3 to 295·9 cm. on the red scale, and from 20·4 to 365·8 cm. on the blue scale. There has evidently been no attempt here to apply the Modulor to the determination of the dimensions of the building as a whole.

In this example at least, the use of the Modulor shows exactly the same limitations which we found in Palladio's system. It integrates the whole structure in the sense that it links the parts to each other, but it fails to relate them to the whole. We have already seen that without its subdivisions the Modulor possesses rather a limited range of additive properties. While this does not matter when it is used to obtain 'textural' unity only, it is probable that to obtain unity in the wider sense the use of the subdivisions would become more important. However, even in the simpler

---

[1] *The Modulor*, p. 37. [2] *Ibid*. p. 43.
[3] *Ibid*. p. 78. [4] *Ibid*. p. 140.

form in which Corbusier has described it, the Modulor shows the enormous value of a system of proportion based, not on complicated geometrical constructions or arithmetical calculations, but on the manipulation of the sort of instrument with which the present-day architect is most at home, the scale.

Finally, Corbusier raises a question to which he does not attempt to give a final answer: '. . .assuming that the "Modulor" is the key to the "door of the miracle of numbers", if only in a very limited sphere, is that door merely one of a hundred or a thousand miraculous doors which may or do exist in that sphere, or have we, by sheer hazard, opened the one and only door that was waiting to be discovered?'[1] The answer to this question seems to be that there are not likely to be many doors, and only a few have been discovered; the Modulor, based as it is on the ϕ series, provides a key to one of the best of them.

[1] *The Modulor*, pp. 62–3.

CHAPTER VII

CONCLUSION

We have now completed our survey of the history of the theory of proportion in architecture, and of the different practical systems which have been put forward from time to time. We have seen again and again that, however the various theories differ on the surface, their contradictions disappear when they are translated into terms of the theory which was outlined at the start. This is the theory that the object of proportion is the creation of order apparent to the eye by the repetition of similar figures, and that this is accompanied by the generation of patterns of relationships of mathematical proportion between the linear dimensions of the design. Of these patterns of proportional relationships, the geometric progression is typical.

We have noticed the development of various types of practical systems of proportion. The most important of these historically have been the analytical system using commensurable ratios, and the geometrical system using incommensurable ratios. We found in Vitruvius a possible explanation of the ancient origin of analytical and commensurable systems. These may have developed from the systems of measurement necessary for the practice of arts, which, like architecture, require the co-operation of many men. In their early forms these systems of measurement made use of many measures, often borrowed from the parts of the human body, and related to each other by simple ratios.

We have suspected that systems of this type competed with other systems, geometrical and incommensurable, which would be developed separately in the practice of the more individual arts of pottery, painting and sculpture. In these arts the manipulation of shapes is under the direct control of one man, and the need for systems of measurement is less. Instead, attention could be turned to the geometrical problem of the repetition of similar shapes.

In the closely related field of symmetry, where the problem is that of the repetition of identical figures, generation after generation of artists experimented through the centuries of comparatively stable civilization in Egypt. It is now realized that these Egyptian artists arrived by purely empirical methods at a practical knowledge of symmetry thousands of years before a full theoretical understanding of it became possible.[1]

[1] 'There are 17 essentially different kinds of symmetry possible for a two-dimensional ornament with double infinite rapport. Examples for all 17 groups of symmetry are found among the decorative patterns of

It is unlikely that the same artists failed to apply their imagination and inventiveness in the field of proportion as well. Perhaps they discovered through generations of experiment that certain kinds of rectangles like the root-rectangles and the ϕ and θ rectangles were more suitable for arrangement in proportional patterns than others. This, at any rate, is the implication of Hambidge's reconstruction of Egyptian and Greek methods of design.

All of this is based on indirect evidence. By the time the first surviving account of proportional theory came to be written by Vitruvius, analytical and commensurable systems had become dominant, although fragments of a geometrical and incommensurable system seem to survive in his reference to the $\sqrt{2}$ rectangle. The use of geometry reappeared in the Middle Ages, but the little evidence which exists scarcely shows that this ever developed into a very complete or consistent system of proportion. Analytical and commensurable systems again became dominant in the Renaissance through the influence of Vitruvius. But these systems tended to be confined within the rather narrow framework of the 'musical analogy', possibly through the interpretation of Vitruvius in terms of neo-Platonism, and were open to serious criticism which reached a climax in the eighteenth century. Then nineteenth-century archaeology restored the interest in the geometrical and incommensurable, which again entered into competition with the analytical and commensurable.

Analytical systems, based on the use of the measuring rod, are of the greatest practical convenience in architecture. They also simplify the study of the mathematical relationships with which the designer is concerned, by reducing the problem of proportion from two or three dimensions to one. But they achieve their results indirectly through the manipulation of ratios, and difficulties of arithmetic have tended in the past to exclude the use of incommensurable ratios.

Geometrical systems are in some ways less convenient for the architect, and the mathematical relationships with which the designer is concerned are extremely intricate. But they rely on the direct manipulation of similar shapes, and, as they can handle the incommensurable just as easily as the commensurable, they can take advantage of the valuable properties of numbers like ϕ and θ.

antiquity, in particular among the Egyptian ornaments. One can hardly overestimate the depth of geometric imagination and inventiveness reflected in these patterns. Their construction is far from being mathematically trivial. The art of ornament contains in implicit form the oldest piece of higher mathematics known to us. To be sure, the conceptual means for a complete abstract formulation of the underlying problem, namely the mathematical notion of a group of transformations, was not provided before the nineteenth century; and only on this basis is one able to prove that the 17 symmetries already implicitly known to the Egyptian craftsmen exhaust all possibilities. Strangely enough the proof was carried out only as late.as 1924 by George Pólya...' (Hermann Weyl, *Symmetry* (Princeton University Press, 1952), pp. 103–4).

Progress can lie either in the direction of simplifying geometry, on the lines adopted by Harry Roberts, or in the direction of perfecting the analytical type of system. The work of Schooling, Hambidge and Corbusier has shown how an analytical system can be made to handle incommensurable ratios, and take advantage of the flexibility provided, for instance, by the wide range of additive properties of the ϕ series. This type of system, incommensurable as well as analytical, seems to combine the advantages of the main systems of the past.

For the present-day architect the analytical method has even greater advantages than it had for his predecessors. For them it simplified the problem of organizing the execution of a design to have a convenient method of expressing linear dimensions. Today dimensional requirements play a much more important part in the architectural programme itself, and the architect is very much more at home with a scale than with any other instrument.

In our study of the Modulor we found that, in the form in which it has usually been described, it can be used to create 'textural' unity of detail, but not, perhaps, to relate the parts of a design to the whole. For this purpose the addition of subdivisions to the scales would become a matter of importance. Another development lies in the possibility of using the Fibonacci series as a substitute for the ϕ series. We have seen that in the English version of the Modulor the working dimensions are based on a 'module' of half an inch. There is no reason why this should not be replaced by 4 inches or any other small and convenient unit, so that the practical advantages of 'modular co-ordination' could be combined with the aesthetic advantages of an effective system of proportion.

We have noticed how Sir Edwin Lutyens gave up using the ϕ rectangle in order to take advantage of certain valuable properties of the $\sqrt{2}$ rectangle. It would be well worth exploring the possibility of using a proportional scale based not, like Corbusier's Modulor, on the ϕ series, but on the closely related θ series. Here again the dimensions could be made commensurable by the use of Pell's series as a substitute for the θ series. It would also be possible to develop an analytical method using neither the ϕ series nor the θ series, but the triple geometric progression based on the numbers $\sqrt{3}$, $1 + \sqrt{3}$ and 2.

But a more detailed investigation of these possibilities would fall outside the scope of the present discussion. We set ourselves the task of stating a theory of proportion which would explain the history of proportion in terms, not of metaphysical systems, but of simple relationships of form which are apparent to the eye. We cannot proceed any further here with the next step. This is the application of the theory of proportion to the perfection of practical systems, whose aim is to aid the designer in his task of bringing delight to the human eye.

APPENDIX

The following examples illustrate some simple problems in proportion. Only the solutions of the problems are given, and the straightforward but tedious analysis on which the solutions are based has been omitted. This type of exhaustive analysis of any but the simplest problem in proportion is a very lengthy task, and quite out of the question in practical design. The examples are intended to give an insight into the way in which economy of form can be achieved through the repetition of similar shapes, and to provide material for developing the theory of proportion.

Two simplifications are introduced. The discussion is restricted to problems in two dimensions, and to problems involving patterns of rectangles only. As a matter of fact most of the problems with which the architect has to deal are of this comparatively simple type.

Some sort of notation is required to describe the proportional relationships which arise in the solution of the problems. A number of different methods have been invented for this type of analysis. The similarity of shape of different rectangles can be indicated in some geometrical manner, such as drawing their diagonals, but this only shows the qualitative nature of the relationships. Another method, used by Hambidge, is to express the dimensions of the rectangles and the ratios of their sides in decimal notation. This, however, has the disadvantage of concealing mathematical relationships which could be made obvious. Here we shall try to show the proportional relationships occurring in the examples quantitatively as well as qualitatively by the following method.

Square roots will be indicated by the usual symbols, $\sqrt{2}$, $\sqrt{3}$, etc. The number $1\cdot618\ldots$, or $\dfrac{1+\sqrt{5}}{2}$, will be indicated by the symbol ϕ. Another important but less familiar number, $2\cdot414\ldots$, or $1+\sqrt{2}$, will be indicated by the symbol θ. Further, it will usually be convenient to make the smallest dimension of a diagram equal to one unit of length. The term 'axis of symmetry' will be used in the normal sense to describe the line along which a plane of symmetry intersects a diagram, and not in the mathematical sense of an axis of rotational symmetry.

Fig. 1a

Example 1. Fig. 1a shows a rectangle divided into two parts. All three shapes, that of the whole and the two parts, are different.

There are three ways of eliminating one of the shapes. We may make either part similar in shape to the whole (fig. 1b). We may make the two parts similar in shape to each other, but

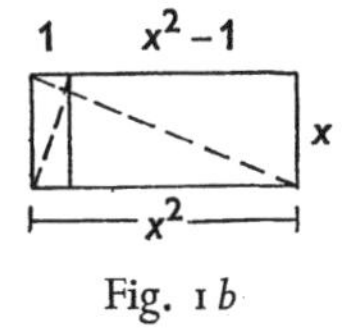

Fig. 1b

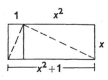

Fig. 1c

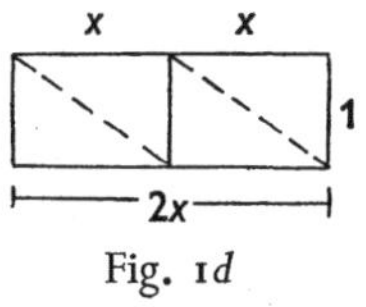

Fig. 1d

different in size (fig. 1c). Finally, we may make the two parts identical. In this case the result is symmetrical (fig. 1d). None of these cases is unique, as we can give the dimension x in the diagrams any value we wish.

There is, however, only one way of eliminating two of the three shapes (fig. 1e). In this case the ratio of the sides of all three rectangles is $\sqrt{2}:1$, and the rectangles can be described as $\sqrt{2}$ rectangles. This is the only case where all the parts of a design can be made similar in shape to the whole.

A great deal can be learnt even from this extremely simple example. In figs. 1b and c two of the rectangles have been made similar in shape by the use of continued proportion. Of the four linear dimensions of the diagrams, three form the geometric progression $1, x, x^2$. In fig. 1d two of the rectangles have been made not only similar in shape but also identical by the simpler and more obvious method of making two of the linear dimensions equal. In fig. 1e the highest possible degree of proportion has been reached

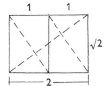

Fig. 1e

by a combination of both methods. Not only are two of the dimensions equal, but all of them belong to the geometric progression $1, \sqrt{2}, 2$. The possibility of the solution depends on the fact that this geometric progression has the additive property $1 + 1 = 2$. This fact may appear trivial in the present case, but it is an example of an important principle.

Example 2. Fig. 2a shows a rectangle divided horizontally and vertically. It consists of nine rectangles of different shapes: the whole, the two rectangles into which it is divided vertically, the two rectangles into which it is divided horizontally, and the four small rectangles.

Fig. 2a

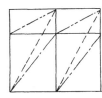

Fig. 2b

Although this diagram is extremely simple, an exhaustive list of the different ways in which the number of shapes can be reduced would be very long. It will shorten the list to consider only solutions based on various types of symmetry. This is not intended to suggest that many effective asymmetrical solutions are not possible.

In fig. 2b, one of the divisions has been made central. It has therefore become an axis of symmetry. As a result three pairs of rectangles are identical, and the number of different shapes has been reduced from nine to six.

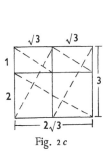

Fig. 2c

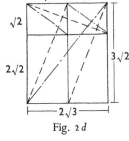

Fig. 2d

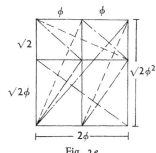

Fig. 2e

There are about twenty different ways of reducing the number of shapes still further without introducing a higher degree of symmetry, but of these only three reduce the number to as few as three. These are shown in figs. 2c, d and e.

In fig. 2c there are five different linear dimensions, of which three, 1, $\sqrt{3}$ and 3, are in continued proportion. The remaining two, 2 and $2\sqrt{3}$, are related to 1 and $\sqrt{3}$ by simple proportion. These mathematical relationships may be indicated thus:

$$1 \quad \sqrt{3} \quad 3$$
$$2 \quad 2\sqrt{3}$$

The mathematical relationships of the five dimensions in fig. 2d are very similar:

$$\sqrt{2} \quad \sqrt{3}$$
$$2\sqrt{2} \quad 2\sqrt{3} \quad 3\sqrt{2}$$

Fig. 2e shows a curious combination of $\sqrt{2}$ rectangles and the golden section. Of the five different dimensions, two groups of three are in continued proportion, with one dimension in common. This arrangement can be indicated thus:

$$\phi$$
$$\sqrt{2} \quad \sqrt{2}\phi \quad \sqrt{2}\phi^2$$
$$2\phi$$

The solution is made possible by the important additive property of the geometric progression 1, ϕ, ϕ^2, ..., i.e. $1 + \phi = \phi^2$.

Fig. 2f

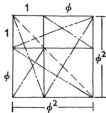

Fig. 2g

The preceding diagrams have had one vertical axis of symmetry, which might equally well have been horizontal. Fig. 2f has one diagonal axis of symmetry. The shape of the whole and of two of the parts is a square. In this case the number of shapes is four. There is only one way of reducing this number without increasing the degree of symmetry. This depends again on the use of the golden section, and is shown in fig. 2g.

In fig. 2g the number of shapes is reduced to three. There are only three different dimensions, 1, ϕ and ϕ^2, which are in continued proportion. This provides another and simpler illustration of the additive property: $1 + \phi = \phi^2$.

If instead of one axis of symmetry two, vertical and horizontal, are used, the number of different shapes is reduced to three (fig. 2h). The four small rectangles become the same shape as the whole, and the four remaining rectangles become two identical pairs. The dimensions are reduced by repetition to four in simple proportion:

$$1 \quad 2$$
$$a \quad 2a$$

The number of rectangles can be reduced to two by making the whole a $\sqrt{2}$ rectangle (fig. 2 i). In this case the four dimensions are in continued proportion:

$$1 \quad \sqrt{2} \quad 2 \quad 2\sqrt{2}.$$

As in fig. 1e the solution depends on the simple additive properties:

$$1 + 1 = 2, \quad \sqrt{2} + \sqrt{2} = 2\sqrt{2}.$$

Finally, the highest degree of symmetry which can be applied in this example, or in any other based on patterns of rectangles, is obtained by the use of four axes of symmetry (fig. 2j). In this case the whole and the four small parts become squares, and the remaining rectangles are double squares. The number of shapes is therefore two.

There is no way of reducing the number of shapes to one.

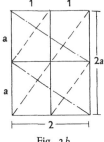

Fig. 2h

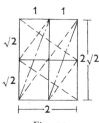

Fig. 2i

Fig. 2j

Example 2 has illustrated the two methods of reducing the number of shapes in a design. The first method consists in the repetition of identical figures. In some cases this leads automatically to the repetition of similar figures as well, as in figs. 2f–i. The second method requires the use of linear dimensions related by mathematical proportion, and particularly by continued proportion. Further, the example has shown the effectiveness of the use of geometric progressions with additive properties. The example has shown the use of various types of symmetry alone, and of symmetry combined with mathematical proportion. By considering even more solutions, it would have been possible to show the use of mathematical proportion alone. While this is perhaps unnecessary, one or two further examples are still required to bring out some other points.

Example 3. Fig. 3a shows a rectangle divided by two horizontal and two vertical divisions. From this simple diagram it is possible to pick out rectangles of thirty-six different shapes, and there is evidently a great deal of room for the introduction of order.

It may be objected at this point that not all the rectangles are of equal importance to the eye. This is evidently true, and the rectangles of most obvious importance are the containing rectangle and the nine small ones. In practice other rectangles might be stressed by emphasis on their boundaries, by the use of colour, or in other ways. In the present discussion it will be simplest, however, to study the methods of reducing the total number of rectangles, without considering their relative importance.

Fig. 3a

In this example there are very many ways of introducing order, using different types of symmetry, mathematical proportion, or a combination of both. The only solutions considered will be based on the highest degree of symmetry possible in this case.

Fig. 3 b shows a solution of this type, with vertical, horizontal, and two diagonal axes of symmetry. The order at once introduced is very obvious to the eye, and this corresponds to the fact that the number of shapes has been reduced from thirty-six to seven.

There are six different ways of reducing the number of shapes still further, of which five rely on mathematical proportion. Figs. 3 c, d and e show the methods of reducing the number to six, a rather unimpressive achievement. In all three cases three of the four different dimensions are in continued proportion. The remaining dimension has no proportional relationship to the others:

fig. 3 c:　1, 2, 4, with 3 excluded;

fig. 3 d:　1, ϕ, ϕ^2, with $\sqrt{5}\phi$ excluded;

fig. 3 e:　1, θ, θ^2, with $\sqrt{2}\theta$ excluded.

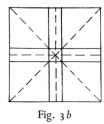

Fig. 3 b

Fig. 3 c

Fig. 3 d

Fig. 3 e

Fig. 3 d illustrates, in addition to the well-known additive property $1 + \phi = \phi^2$, the less familiar fact that $2 + \phi = 1 + \phi^2 = \sqrt{5}\phi$. Fig. 3 e introduces the geometric progression 1, θ, θ^2,.... The number θ, or $1 + \sqrt{2}$, has received very little attention from anyone but mathematicians, although it plays the same part in Hambidge's $\sqrt{2}$ geometry that the number ϕ plays in his $\sqrt{5}$ geometry. The peculiar properties of ϕ and θ will be taken for granted for the time being.

Fig. 3 f shows the only method of reducing the number of shapes to five, and provides another illustration of the use of the number θ. All four dimensions are related by simple proportion:

$$1 \qquad \theta$$
$$\sqrt{2} \quad \sqrt{2}\theta$$

Figs. 3 g and h show the two ways of reducing the number of shapes to four, and exhibit the highest degree of order which is possible in this example.

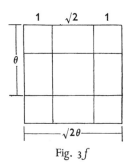

Fig. 3 f

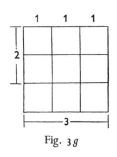

Fig. 3 g

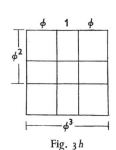

Fig. 3 h

Fig. 3 g represents an imperfect form of the translational symmetry of the repeat pattern. There are no proportional relationships between the three different dimensions, 1, 2 and 3, and it is simply their small number which accounts for the small number of shapes.

In fig. 3 h, on the other hand, there are four different dimensions, 1, ϕ, ϕ^2 and ϕ^3, and it is the fact that they are in continued proportion which accounts for the small number of shapes.

From the point of view which has been adopted in this discussion, figs. 3 g and h show exactly the same degree of order. It might be considered that fig. 3 h, based on mathematical proportion, is more interesting to the eye than fig. 3 g, based on repeat symmetry.

Example 3 has introduced the use of the number θ, and of repeat symmetry. One more example will be given.

Example 4. Fig. 4 a shows a rectangle with four vertical and four horizontal divisions drawn at random. The total number of shapes which can be picked out is 225. No doubt many of the shapes are indistinguishable to the eye, and if they were arranged in order there would in many cases be an almost imperceptible transition from one clearly recognizable shape to another. This state of affairs is perhaps even more confusing to the eye than a large number of clearly defined shapes.

Fig. 4 b shows the same arrangement with the highest possible degree of symmetry introduced. The number of shapes is reduced from 225 to 37, a considerable achievement.

Fig. 4 a

Fig. 4 b

An exhaustive study of the methods of introducing a still higher degree of order has not been attempted, but the two solutions which appear to be the most effective are given.

Fig. 4 c shows a solution using the number θ, which in this example seems to be more effective than the number ϕ. The total number of shapes has been reduced to 11. The seven different dimensions can be arranged in three overlapping groups of three in continued proportion:

$$1 \qquad \theta \qquad \theta^2$$
$$\sqrt{2} \quad \sqrt{2\theta} \quad \sqrt{2\theta^2}$$
$$2\theta$$

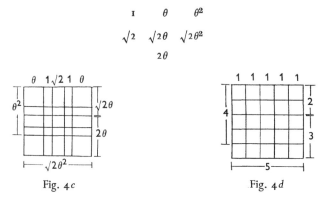

Fig. 4 c

Fig. 4 d

Fig. 4 d shows the most effective solution, with only ten different shapes. It is another example of repeat symmetry. There are only five dimensions, 1, 2, 3, 4 and 5, of which 1, 2 and 4 are in continued proportion. This figure shows a slightly higher degree of order than the previous one, but it achieves this at the expense of some loss of interest in the pattern.

B. PATTERNS OF PROPORTIONAL RELATIONSHIPS

The examples have illustrated a variety of patterns of proportional relationships:

1. Simple proportion 1 a figs. $2h$; $3f$.

                               b ab

2. Continued proportion 1 a a^2 figs. $1b, c, e$; $2g$; $3c, d, e$.

                            1 a a^2 a^3 figs. $2i$; $3h$.

3. Simple and continued 1 a a^2 figs. $2c, d$.

      proportion combined b ab

                                a

                             b ab a^2b fig. $2e$.

                             ab^2

                             1 a a^2

                             b ab a^2b fig. $4c$.

                             ab^2

All these patterns can be regarded as partial expressions of the double geometric progression:

$$
\begin{array}{llll}
1 & a & a^2 & a^3 & \ldots \\
b & ab & a^2b & a^3b & \ldots \\
b^2 & ab^2 & a^2b^2 & a^3b^2 & \ldots \\
b^3 & ab^3 & a^2b^3 & a^3b^3 & \ldots \\
\vdots & \vdots & \vdots & \vdots &
\end{array}
$$

The horizontal, vertical and diagonal lines are all in continued proportion.
The double geometric progression is clearly a combination of the single progressions:

$$
\begin{array}{llllll}
1 & a & a^2 & a^3 & a^4 & \ldots \\
1 & b & b^2 & b^3 & b^4 & \ldots
\end{array}
$$

The part played by the single geometric progression in proportion will already be clear from the examples, and can be explained very easily. Dimensions which are related by this simple pattern of proportional relationships can be used to construct a series of rectangles of the same shape, but of different sizes, e.g.

   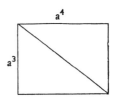

Even if these dimensions are used at random, only a limited number of shapes will be produced, restricted to the number of terms of the progression

It will be seen that as well as rectangles of the same shape but of different sizes, the single geometric progression also enables us to construct rectangles of the same size but of different shapes, which thus conform to the third relationship of visual proportion described on p. 5.

The double geometric progression tends, like the single geometric progression, to restrict the number of shapes in a design, but it does so less effectively. The number of different shapes which can be produced is not limited to the number of terms of the progression, but increases more rapidly. The examples have shown, however, that in spite of this disadvantage the double geometric progression is of the greatest importance in proportion. The reasons for this will be explained in the next section.

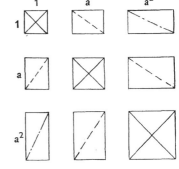

C. ADDITIVE PROPERTIES

The use of a geometric progression enables us to repeat similar shapes in a design. This, however, can be done more effectively if it is possible to add terms of the progression together to obtain other terms. It then becomes possible to add rectangles of the limited series of shapes together to obtain other rectangles belonging to the same series, and to relate small parts of the design to larger parts and to the whole.

Example 1 showed how two $\sqrt{2}$ rectangles can be added together to obtain a third, and how this depends on the fact that the geometric progression 1, $\sqrt{2}$, 2, ... has the additive property $1 + 1 = 2$.

The most valuable type of geometric progression is therefore one with additive properties. A number of these have been encountered in the examples and are given here:

TYPE OF SERIES	SERIES ILLUSTRATED				ADDITIVE PROPERTIES ILLUSTRATED	
Whole numbers	1	2	4	... 3c	$1 + 2 + 1 = 4$	
Square roots	1	$\sqrt{2}$	2	... 1e, 2e, 2i; 4c	$1 + 1 \quad = 2$	$\sqrt{2} + \sqrt{2} = 2\sqrt{2}$
Other numbers	1	ϕ	ϕ^2	... 2e, 2g; 3d, 3h	$1 + \phi \quad = \phi^2$	$1 + 2\phi = \phi^3$
	1	θ	θ^2	... 3e; 4c	$1 + 2\theta \quad = \theta^2$	

Only those additive properties which are actually illustrated in the examples are given.

In many cases the additive properties of a single geometric progression fail to give the best solution, and it is in these cases that groups of dimensions with more complicated proportional relationships occur. For instance the dimensions in fig. 2c show the following pattern of proportional relationships:

$$1 \quad \sqrt{3} \quad 3$$
$$2 \quad 2\sqrt{3}$$

The additive properties illustrated are $1 + 2 = 3$ and $\sqrt{3} + \sqrt{3} = 2\sqrt{3}$.

Fig. 2 *d* shows the following:

$$\sqrt{2} \qquad \sqrt{3}$$

$$2\sqrt{2} \quad 2\sqrt{3} \quad 3\sqrt{2}$$

The proportional relationships can be shown more clearly by writing this as

$$\frac{1}{2} \quad \frac{\sqrt{3}}{2\sqrt{2}}$$

$$1 \qquad \frac{\sqrt{3}}{\sqrt{2}} \quad \frac{3}{2}$$

The additive properties are $\quad \dfrac{1}{2} + 1 = \dfrac{3}{2} \quad$ and $\quad \dfrac{\sqrt{3}}{2\sqrt{2}} + \dfrac{\sqrt{3}}{2\sqrt{2}} = \dfrac{\sqrt{3}}{\sqrt{2}}$.

In fig. 3*f* there are four dimensions in simple proportion:

$$1 \qquad \theta$$

$$\sqrt{2} \quad \sqrt{2\theta}$$

The additive properties are: $\quad 1 + \sqrt{2} = \theta \quad$ and $\quad 1 + \sqrt{2} + 1 = \sqrt{2\theta}$.

Finally, fig. 4*c* shows the following pattern of proportional relationships:

$$1 \qquad \theta \qquad \theta^2$$

$$\sqrt{2} \quad \sqrt{2\theta} \quad \sqrt{2\theta^2}$$

$$2\theta$$

and the following additive properties:

$$1 + \sqrt{2} = \theta$$

$$1 + \sqrt{2} + 1 = \sqrt{2\theta}$$

$$\theta + 1 + \sqrt{2} = 2\theta$$

$$\theta + 1 + \sqrt{2} + 1 = \theta^2$$

$$\theta + 1 + \sqrt{2} + 1 + \theta = \sqrt{2\theta^2}$$

In this case the combination of the two geometric progressions 1, θ, θ^2, ... and 1, $\sqrt{2}$, 2, ... gives a far greater variety of additive properties than that given by either progression alone.

We have already seen that by using multiple geometric progressions we run the risk of adding to the number of shapes in a design unduly. In the last example the danger is avoided because a small number of terms only of the combined progression is used.

Of the single geometric progressions illustrated in the examples, the widest variety of additive properties is provided by the ϕ series, on which several solutions are based. But in more complicated examples it would be found that even the ϕ series is not flexible enough to provide a solution by itself. In practical systems of proportion double or triple progressions occur, or groups of single progressions superimposed like the red and blue scales of Corbusier's Modulor.

137

The whole-number series are very deficient in additive properties, but in spite of this the double geometric progression based on the numbers 2 and 3 was important in the Renaissance. The double geometric progression based on the numbers $\sqrt{2}$ and θ gives a greater variety of additive properties, and is embodied, for instance, in some of the Greek vases analysed by Hambidge and Caskey.[1] But far more of these vases incorporate multiple progressions related to the ϕ series, which give a still greater variety of additive properties, and of which the triple progression based on the numbers 2, $\sqrt{5}$ and ϕ is a typical example.[2]

The solution of individual problems of proportion may make use of the properties of other numbers which have not appeared in our examples. It is unlikely, however, that many of these give rise to progressions with a wide enough range of additive properties to be of much general usefulness, or to form the basis of a system of proportion. An exception to this is the triple progression based on the numbers 2, $\sqrt{3}$ and $1+\sqrt{3}$, which may be generated by the use of the 30°–60° and 45° set-squares, or by the manipulation of equilateral triangles or hexagons.

The next section will be devoted to a more detailed study of the mathematical properties of ϕ and θ.

D. THE NUMBERS ϕ AND θ

Interest in the arithmetic of the number ϕ, as opposed to the geometry of the golden section, arose amongst mathematicians as part of a very small episode in the nineteenth-century history of the theory of numbers. This interest developed not because of the possible applications of the number ϕ in systems of proportion, but because of its connexion with the Fibonacci series, 0, 1, 1, 2, 3, 5, 8, 13, 21, ...

In the same way the mathematicians were interested in the very similar connexion between the number θ and Pell's series, 0, 1, 2, 5, 12, 29, 70, 169, ... They were not, however, primarily interested in the numbers ϕ and θ themselves at this time, and they had no need to invent special symbols for them. The number ϕ was only given its name when its possible value in the theory of proportion was first clearly recognized. It was then given the name ϕ by Mark Barr in honour of Pheidias. So far as the writer is aware the number θ has never received a name, and the symbol θ is therefore an improvisation.

The ϕ series was discussed from the point of view of the theory of proportion by Schooling in an important contribution to Sir Theodore Cook's book *The Curves of Life*, published in 1914. He described a number of its peculiarities, and gave a list of the simple additive properties of the series.

The θ series never seems to have been discussed from this point of view, although we find it appearing from time to time in practice. It may therefore be of interest to compare some of the properties of θ with the comparatively well-known properties of ϕ.

---

[1] E.g. in vase no. 178 in Caskey's *Geometry of Greek Vases* (1922). When Caskey's analysis of this lekythos is translated into terms of $\sqrt{2}$ and θ, the following pattern of proportional relationships comes to light:

$$\begin{array}{cccccc}
\sqrt{2} & 2 & 2\sqrt{2} & 4 & & \\
\sqrt{2}\theta & 2\theta & 2\sqrt{2}\theta & 4\theta & 4\sqrt{2}\theta & \\
\theta^2 & \sqrt{2}\theta^2 & 2\theta^2 & 2\sqrt{2}\theta^2 & 4\theta^2 & 4\sqrt{2}\theta^2 \\
& \sqrt{2}\theta^3 & & 2\sqrt{2}\theta^3 & &
\end{array}$$

[2] This progression can be found, for instance, in the proportions of a neck amphora illustrated by Caskey (vase no. 18) and Hambidge (*Dynamic Symmetry*, p. 129, fig. 8).

1. ϕ is the positive solution of the equation

$$x^2 = x + 1.$$

$$\phi = \frac{1 + \sqrt{5}}{2}$$

$$= 1 \cdot 618\ldots$$

$$= 1 + \cfrac{1}{1 + \cfrac{1}{1 + \ldots}}$$

θ is the positive solution of the equation

$$x^2 = 2x + 1.$$

$$\theta = 1 + \sqrt{2}$$

$$= 2 \cdot 414\ldots$$

$$= 2 + \cfrac{1}{2 + \cfrac{1}{2 + \ldots}}$$

2. The rectangle whose sides are in the ratio $1 : \phi$, i.e. the ratio of the golden section, is described by Ghyka as the ϕ rectangle. This is convenient and concise, and makes clear its relationship with other rectangles which can be described as the ϕ^2, ϕ^3 rectangles, etc.

Hambidge calls the ϕ rectangle the 1·618 rectangle, or the 'whirling square' rectangle, because of the pattern of squares which is produced by a spiral arrangement of ϕ rectangles.

The rectangle whose sides are in the ratio $1 : \theta$ can conveniently be called the θ rectangle.

Where Hambidge refers to it he calls the θ rectangle the 2·414 rectangle. He could also have called it the 'whirling double square' rectangle.

In *Dynamic Symmetry* and *The Elements of Dynamic Symmetry* Hambidge illustrates many geometrical properties of the ϕ rectangle and some of those of the θ rectangle. A few of these are given below.

3. A $\sqrt{5}$ rectangle can be divided into a square and two ϕ rectangles.

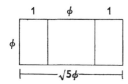

A $\sqrt{2}$ rectangle can be divided into a square and one θ rectangle.

4. A ϕ rectangle can be divided into two squares and two $\sqrt{5}$ rectangles.

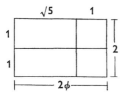

A θ rectangle can be divided into one square and one $\sqrt{2}$ rectangle.

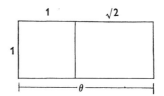

5. A ϕ rectangle can be divided into a square and a ϕ rectangle.

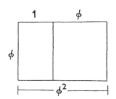

6. A ϕ rectangle and a square can be arranged to form a ϕ^2 rectangle.

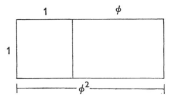

7. The important part played by the ratio $1 : \phi$ in the geometry of the pentagon and star pentagon or 'pentagram' is well known.

Macody Lund attached great importance to the way in which an expanding series of star pentagons gives the ϕ series.

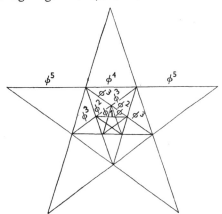

8. The simple additive properties of the ϕ series are well known:

$$\phi^2 = 1 + \phi, \qquad \phi^3 = 1 + 2\phi, \qquad \phi^4 = 2 + 3\phi,$$
$$\phi^5 = 3 + 5\phi, \qquad \phi^6 = 5 + 8\phi, \qquad \ldots$$

The whole numbers which appear as coefficients belong to the Fibonacci series.

A θ rectangle can be divided into two squares and a θ rectangle.

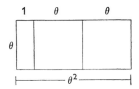

Two θ rectangles and a square can be arranged to form a θ^2 rectangle.

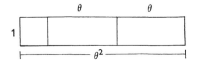

The ratio $1 : \theta$ plays a similar part in the geometry of the octagon and star octagon.

An expanding series of star octagons will give the θ series in a rather similar manner.

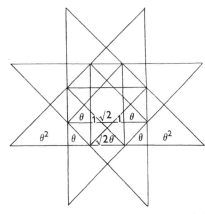

The simple additive properties of the θ series are similar:

$$\theta^2 = 1 + 2\theta, \qquad \theta^3 = 2 + 5\theta, \qquad \theta^4 = 5 + 12\theta,$$
$$\theta^5 = 12 + 29\theta, \qquad \theta^6 = 29 + 70\theta, \qquad \ldots$$

The whole numbers which appear as coefficients belong to Pell's series.

APPENDIX

These lists of simple additive properties only include a few of those which are important in practice. A more complete statement of the additive properties of these series is given below.

9. The Fibonacci series has the property that the ratio of successive pairs of its terms tends to ϕ. Its terms have the same additive properties as those of the ϕ series, so for many purposes it can be used as a substitute for the ϕ series.

Pell's series has the property that the ratio of successive pairs of its terms tends to θ. Its terms have the same additive properties as those of the θ series, so for many purposes it can be used as a substitute for the θ series.

10. By an extension of this principle we can replace the double progression

$$
\begin{array}{cccc}
1 & \phi & \phi^2 & \dots \\
\sqrt{5} & \sqrt{5}\phi & \sqrt{5}\phi^2 & \dots \\
5 & 5\phi & 5\phi^2 & \dots
\end{array}
$$

by the composite series

$$
\begin{array}{ccccccccc}
0 & 1 & 1 & 2 & 3 & 5 & 8 & \dots \\
2 & 1 & 3 & 4 & 7 & 11 & 18 & \dots \\
0 & 5 & 5 & 10 & 15 & 25 & 40 & \dots
\end{array}
$$

By an extension of this principle we can replace the double progression

$$
\begin{array}{cccc}
1 & \theta & \theta^2 & \dots \\
\sqrt{2} & \sqrt{2}\theta & \sqrt{2}\theta^2 & \dots \\
2 & 2\theta & 2\theta^2 & \dots
\end{array}
$$

by the composite series

$$
\begin{array}{cccccccc}
0 & 1 & 2 & 5 & 12 & 29 & 70 & \dots \\
1 & 1 & 3 & 7 & 17 & 41 & 99 & \dots \\
0 & 2 & 4 & 10 & 24 & 58 & 140 & \dots
\end{array}
$$

E. ADDITIVE PROPERTIES OF THE ϕ AND θ SERIES

The θ series

TABLE A

$$
\begin{array}{llll}
\theta^2 = 1 + 2\theta & 5\theta^2 = 1 + 2\theta^3 & 12\theta^2 = 2 + 2\theta^4 & 29\theta^2 = 5 + 2\theta^5 \; \dots \\
\theta^3 = 2 + 5\theta & & & \\
\theta^4 = 5 + 12\theta & 5\theta^4 = 1 + 12\theta^3 & & 29\theta^4 = 1 + 12\theta^5 \; \dots \\
\theta^5 = 12 + 29\theta & 5\theta^5 = 2 + 29\theta^3 & & \\
\quad \dots & \quad \dots & & \quad \dots
\end{array}
$$

TABLE B

$$
\begin{array}{lllll}
\sqrt{2}\theta = 1 + \theta & 2\sqrt{2}\theta = 1 + \theta^2 & 5\sqrt{2}\theta = 3 + \theta^3 & 12\sqrt{2}\theta = 7 + \theta^4 & 29\sqrt{2}\theta = 17 + \theta^5 \; \dots \\
\sqrt{2}\theta^2 = 1 + 3\theta & & & & \\
\sqrt{2}\theta^3 = 3 + 7\theta & & 5\sqrt{2}\theta^3 = 1 + 7\theta^3 & 12\sqrt{2}\theta^3 = 1 + 7\theta^4 & 29\sqrt{2}\theta^3 = 3 + 7\theta^5 \; \dots \\
\sqrt{2}\theta^4 = 7 + 17\theta & & 5\sqrt{2}\theta^4 = 1 + 17\theta^3 & & \\
\quad \dots & & \quad \dots & & \quad \dots
\end{array}
$$

TABLE C

$$
\begin{array}{llll}
\theta = 1 + \sqrt{2} & & & \\
\theta^2 = 3 + 2\sqrt{2} & 3\theta^2 = 1 + 2\sqrt{2}\theta^2 & 7\theta^2 = 1 + 2\sqrt{2}\theta^3 & 17\theta^2 = 3 + 2\sqrt{2}\theta^4 \; \dots \\
\theta^3 = 7 + 5\sqrt{2} & 3\theta^3 = 1 + 5\sqrt{2}\theta^2 & & \\
\theta^4 = 17 + 12\sqrt{2} & 3\theta^4 = 3 + 12\sqrt{2}\theta^2 & & 17\theta^4 = 1 + 12\sqrt{2}\theta^4 \; \dots \\
\quad \dots & \quad \dots & & \quad \dots
\end{array}
$$

TABLE D

$$\theta = \sqrt{2}+1 \qquad 3\theta = \sqrt{2}+\theta^2 \qquad 7\theta = 2\sqrt{2}+\theta^3 \qquad 17\theta = 5\sqrt{2}+\theta^4 \ \ldots$$
$$\theta^2 = 2\sqrt{2}+3$$
$$\theta^3 = 5\sqrt{2}+7 \qquad 3\theta^3 = \sqrt{2}+7\theta^2 \qquad\qquad\qquad 17\theta^3 = \sqrt{2}+7\theta^4 \ \ldots$$
$$\theta^4 = 12\sqrt{2}+17 \qquad 3\theta^4 = 2\sqrt{2}+17\theta^2$$
$$\ldots \qquad\qquad \ldots \qquad\qquad\qquad\qquad \ldots$$

These tables can of course be extended in both directions. The part played by the whole-number series o, 1, 2, 5, 12, ... and 1, 1, 3, 7, 17, ... is obvious.

The ϕ series

TABLE A

$$\phi^2 = 1+\phi \qquad 2\phi^2 = 1+\phi^3 \qquad 3\phi^2 = 1+\phi^4 \qquad 5\phi^2 = 2+\phi^5 \ \ldots$$
$$\phi^3 = 1+2\phi$$
$$\phi^4 = 2+3\phi \qquad 2\phi^4 = 1+3\phi^3 \qquad\qquad\qquad 5\phi^4 = 1+3\phi^5 \ \ldots$$
$$\phi^5 = 3+5\phi \qquad 2\phi^5 = 1+5\phi^3$$
$$\phi^6 = 5+8\phi \qquad 2\phi^6 = 2+8\phi^3 \qquad\qquad\qquad 5\phi^6 = 1+8\phi^5 \ \ldots$$
$$\ldots \qquad\qquad \ldots \qquad\qquad\qquad\qquad \ldots$$

TABLE B

$$\sqrt{5}\phi = 2+\phi = 1+\phi^2 \qquad 2\sqrt{5}\phi = 3+\phi^3 \qquad 3\sqrt{5}\phi = 4+\phi^4 \qquad 5\sqrt{5}\phi = 7+\phi^5 \ \ldots$$
$$\sqrt{5}\phi^2 = 1+3\phi$$
$$\sqrt{5}\phi^3 = 3+4\phi \qquad 2\sqrt{5}\phi^3 = 2+4\phi^3 \qquad 3\sqrt{5}\phi^3 = 1+4\phi^4 \qquad 5\sqrt{5}\phi^3 = 3+4\phi^5 \ \ldots$$
$$\sqrt{5}\phi^4 = 4+7\phi \qquad 2\sqrt{5}\phi^4 = 1+7\phi^3$$
$$\sqrt{5}\phi^5 = 7+11\phi \qquad 2\sqrt{5}\phi^5 = 3+11\phi^3 \qquad\qquad\qquad 5\sqrt{5}\phi^5 = 2+11\phi^5 \ \ldots$$
$$\ldots \qquad\qquad \ldots \qquad\qquad\qquad\qquad \ldots$$

TABLE C

$$2\phi = 1+\sqrt{5}$$
$$2\phi^2 = 3+\sqrt{5} \qquad 3\phi^2 = 2+\sqrt{5}\phi^2 \qquad 4\phi^2 = 1+\sqrt{5}\phi^3 \qquad 7\phi^2 = 3+\sqrt{5}\phi^4 \ \ldots$$
$$2\phi^3 = 4+2\sqrt{5} \qquad 3\phi^3 = 1+2\sqrt{5}\phi^2$$
$$2\phi^4 = 7+3\sqrt{5} \qquad 3\phi^4 = 3+3\sqrt{5}\phi^2 \qquad\qquad\qquad 7\phi^4 = 2+3\sqrt{5}\phi^4 \ \ldots$$
$$2\phi^5 = 11+5\sqrt{5} \qquad 3\phi^5 = 4+5\sqrt{5}\phi^2 \qquad\qquad\qquad 7\phi^5 = 1+5\sqrt{5}\phi^4$$
$$\ldots \qquad\qquad \ldots \qquad\qquad\qquad\qquad \ldots$$

TABLE D

$$2\phi = \sqrt{5}+1 \qquad 3\phi = \sqrt{5}+\phi^2 \qquad 4\phi = \sqrt{5}+\phi^3 \qquad 7\phi = 2\sqrt{5}+\phi^4 \ \ldots$$
$$2\phi^2 = \sqrt{5}+3$$
$$2\phi^3 = 2\sqrt{5}+4 \qquad 3\phi^3 = \sqrt{5}+4\phi^2 \qquad\qquad\qquad 7\phi^3 = \sqrt{5}+4\phi^4 \ \ldots$$
$$2\phi^4 = 3\sqrt{5}+7 \qquad 3\phi^4 = \sqrt{5}+7\phi^2$$
$$2\phi^5 = 5\sqrt{5}+11 \qquad 3\phi^5 = 2\sqrt{5}+11\phi^2 \qquad\qquad\qquad 7\phi^5 = \sqrt{5}+11\phi^4 \ \ldots$$
$$\ldots \qquad\qquad \ldots \qquad\qquad\qquad\qquad \ldots$$

142

The part played by the whole-number series 0, 1, 1, 2, 3, 5, ... and 2, 1, 3, 4, 7, 11, ... is obvious. The pattern of these tables could be made even clearer by filling in the gaps with equations such as $3\phi^2 = 3\phi^2$, which is of no interest, or $\phi^4 = -1 + 3\phi^2$, which appears elsewhere in the form $3\phi^2 = 1 + \phi^4$.

Certain of the equations can be simplified, and some of these can be arranged in a supplementary table:

$$1 + 1 = 2 \qquad\qquad \phi^4 + 1 = 3\phi^2 \qquad\qquad \phi^8 + 1 = 7\phi^4 \qquad \cdots$$
$$\phi^2 = 1 + \phi \qquad\qquad \phi^6 = 1 + 4\phi^3 \qquad\qquad \phi^{10} = 1 + 11\phi^5 \qquad \cdots$$
$$1 = 1 + 0 \qquad\qquad \phi^4 = 1 + \sqrt{5}\phi^2 \qquad\qquad \phi^8 = 1 + 3\sqrt{5}\phi^4 \qquad \cdots$$
$$\phi^2 + 1 = \sqrt{5}\phi \qquad\qquad \phi^6 + 1 = 2\sqrt{5}\phi^3 \qquad\qquad \phi^{10} + 1 = 5\sqrt{5}\phi^5 \qquad \cdots$$

Apart from their value in analysis, an inspection of these tables can provide a good deal of useful information. In the first place it is clear that the most useful additive properties in practice will be the simplest. Architects are unlikely to care to burden their memories with equations like $7\phi^5 = \sqrt{5} + 11\phi^4$, and the occasions for using such a formula are likely to be rare. On the other hand, comparatively simple equations like $2\phi^2 = 1 + \phi^3$ and $\sqrt{5}\phi = 2 + \phi$ represent relationships of dimensions which are constantly arising in practice whenever the golden section is used. It is useful for the purpose of theoretical analysis to be able to express them in mathematical symbols, and in practice other ways of dealing with them can be found.

Now a comparison of the two sets of tables for θ and ϕ will show that there is a rather larger range of fairly simple additive properties involving ϕ than there is of those involving θ. This fact is obviously connected with the fact that the numbers of Pell's series increase more rapidly than those of the Fibonacci series, and this is itself connected with the simple fact that θ is bigger than ϕ. We have therefore some grounds for believing that systems of proportion based on the properties of the number ϕ are likely to be more flexible in practice than systems of proportion based on the properties of the number θ. These grounds are not, however, strong enough to make us lose our interest in θ altogether, as it may turn out to possess advantages for certain purposes which outweigh its apparent disadvantages.

A second thing which the tables of additive properties can do for us is to provide some sort of guide to the comparative flexibility in practice of different combinations of geometric progressions. We have had examples of the usefulness in practice of the double geometric progression

$$
\begin{array}{ccc}
1 & \theta & \theta^2 \ \cdots \\
\sqrt{2} & \sqrt{2}\theta & \sqrt{2}\theta^2 \ \cdots \\
2 & 2\theta & 2\theta^2 \ \cdots
\end{array}
$$

We can now see a reason for this. Whereas the use of the θ series alone would confine us to the additive properties of the first column of Table A, the use of the double geometric progression allows us to use additive properties from the first columns of all the tables.

In the same way we can compare the flexibility of various combinations of progressions which include the ϕ series. If the progression 1, ϕ, ϕ^2, ... is used by itself, the only additive properties which are available are those from the first column of Table A. The pair of progressions 1, ϕ, ϕ^2, ... and 2, 2ϕ, $2\phi^2$, ..., which form the basis of the Modulor, allow us to make use of the additive properties from the second column of Table A as well as the first. The use of the group of progressions

$$
\begin{array}{ccc}
1 & \phi & \phi^2 \ \cdots \\
\sqrt{5} & \sqrt{5}\phi & \sqrt{5}\phi^2 \ \cdots \\
5 & 5\phi & 5\phi^2 \ \cdots
\end{array}
$$

THE THEORY OF PROPORTION IN ARCHITECTURE

makes it possible to use the additive properties from the first and fourth columns of Table A, the first columns of Table B, and some of the additive properties from Tables C and D.

The last group of progressions is of particular interest as it approximates rather closely to a single geometric progression based on the cube root of ϕ. The approximation can be shown as follows:

1	$\phi^{\frac{1}{3}}$	$\phi^{\frac{2}{3}}$	ϕ	$\phi^{\frac{4}{3}}$	$\phi^{\frac{5}{3}}$	ϕ^2
$1\cdot000$	$1\cdot174$	$1\cdot378$	$1\cdot618$	$1\cdot899$	$2\cdot230$	$2\cdot618$ ...
1	$\dfrac{5}{\phi^3}$	$\dfrac{\sqrt5}{\phi}$	ϕ	$\dfrac{5}{\phi^2}$	$\sqrt5$	ϕ^2
$1\cdot000$	$1\cdot180$	$1\cdot382$	$1\cdot618$	$1\cdot910$	$2\cdot236$	$2\cdot618$ ...

These approximations seem to be sufficiently close to be accepted by the eye. They are of the same order of accuracy as the approximations to true harmony which are obtained by the system of equal-temperament tuning in music. This particular group of progressions thus possesses not only the extensive additive properties of a double geometric progression, but also a fairly close approximation to the simple proportional properties of a single geometric progression.

A still more elaborate progression can be obtained by combining the progressions 1, ϕ, ϕ^2 ..., 1, $\sqrt5$, 5, ... and 1, 2, 4, ... This progression has the disadvantage that a large number of shapes is produced. It has, however, the advantage of enormous flexibility. The additive properties which can be used include the first, second and fourth columns of Table A, the first and second columns of Table B, and the first and third columns of Tables C and D.

F. NUMBERS RELATED TO ϕ AND θ

The numbers ϕ and θ are two members of a family of numbers with similar properties. This family consists of all numbers which can be expressed in the form $\dfrac{a+\sqrt{(a^2+4)}}{2}$, where a is a positive whole number. All members of the family are connected in the same way as ϕ and θ to whole number series, and they all give rise to a wide range of additive properties, which can be arranged in tables having the same pattern.

We obtain the number ϕ by putting $a=1$, and the number θ by putting $a=2$; ϕ and θ are therefore the smallest members of the family. We have already found reason to believe that θ is normally less valuable in proportion than ϕ, and that this is connected with the fact that it is larger. It therefore seems likely that still larger members of the family will compare still less favourably with ϕ.

Most of the other members of the family do not, in fact, look very promising. For instance, putting $a=3$ gives the number $\dfrac{3+\sqrt{13}}{2}$. On the other hand putting $a=4$ gives a more interesting result, as the number becomes $2+\sqrt5$, or ϕ^3. As a matter of fact all odd powers of this family of numbers are themselves members of the same family.

The even powers belong to another family, consisting of numbers which can be expressed in the form $\dfrac{a+\sqrt{(a^2-4)}}{2}$, where a is a positive whole number. For example, putting $a=3$ in this expression gives the number $\dfrac{3+\sqrt5}{2}$, or ϕ^2.

Unfortunately this second family of numbers is of very limited value in proportion. To some extent its members behave in the same way as the members of the first family of numbers, but they differ in an important respect. Tables of additive properties for numbers of this type form a different pattern, and the more useful properties are excluded. This fact is apparent, for instance, in the tables for ϕ^2:

TABLE A

$$3\phi^2 = 1 + \phi^4 \qquad 8\phi^2 = 3 + \phi^6 \qquad 21\phi^2 = 8 + \phi^8 \quad \cdots$$
$$8\phi^4 = 1 + 3\phi^6 \qquad 21\phi^4 = 3 + 3\phi^8 \quad \cdots$$
$$21\phi^6 = 1 + 8\phi^8 \quad \cdots$$
$$\cdots$$

TABLE C

$$2\phi^2 = 3 + \sqrt{5} \qquad 3\phi^2 = 2 + \sqrt{5}\phi^2 \qquad 7\phi^2 = 3 + \sqrt{5}\phi^4 \quad \cdots$$
$$2\phi^4 = 7 + 3\sqrt{5} \qquad 3\phi^4 = 3 + 3\sqrt{5}\phi^2 \qquad 7\phi^4 = 2 + 3\sqrt{5}\phi^4 \quad \cdots$$
$$2\phi^6 = 18 + 8\sqrt{5} \qquad 3\phi^6 = 7 + 8\sqrt{5}\phi^2 \qquad 7\phi^6 = 3 + 8\sqrt{5}\phi^4 \quad \cdots$$
$$\cdots \qquad \cdots \qquad \cdots \qquad \cdots$$

TABLE D

$$2\phi^2 = \sqrt{5} + 3$$
$$2\phi^4 = 3\sqrt{5} + 7 \qquad 3\phi^4 = \sqrt{5} + 7\phi^2$$
$$2\phi^6 = 8\sqrt{5} + 18 \qquad 3\phi^6 = 3\sqrt{5} + 18\phi^2 \qquad 7\phi^6 = \sqrt{5} + 18\phi^4$$
$$\cdots \qquad \cdots \qquad \cdots \qquad \cdots$$

Table B and the more useful parts of Table A have disappeared, so there is good reason to think that members of the second family of numbers are less valuable than those of the first.

The first family of numbers is itself merely a branch of a wider family, consisting of all numbers which can be expressed in the form $\dfrac{a + \sqrt{(a^2 + 4b)}}{2}$, where a and b are both positive whole numbers. The members of this family for values of a and b up to 5 are as follows:

	$a = 1$	$a = 2$	$a = 3$	$a = 4$	$a = 5$	
$b = 1$	ϕ	θ	$\dfrac{3 + \sqrt{13}}{2}$	ϕ^3	$\dfrac{5 + \sqrt{29}}{2}$	$\cdots$
$b = 2$	2	$1 + \sqrt{3}$	$\dfrac{3 + \sqrt{17}}{2}$	$2 + \sqrt{6}$	$\dfrac{5 + \sqrt{33}}{2}$	$\cdots$
$b = 3$	$\dfrac{1 + \sqrt{13}}{2}$	3	$\dfrac{3 + \sqrt{21}}{2}$	$2 + \sqrt{7}$	$\dfrac{5 + \sqrt{37}}{2}$	$\cdots$
$b = 4$	$\dfrac{1 + \sqrt{17}}{2}$	2ϕ	4	2θ	$\dfrac{5 + \sqrt{41}}{2}$	$\cdots$
$b = 5$	$\dfrac{1 + \sqrt{21}}{2}$	$1 + \sqrt{6}$	$\dfrac{3 + \sqrt{29}}{2}$	5	$\sqrt{5}\phi^2$	$\cdots$
	$\vdots$	$\vdots$	$\vdots$	$\vdots$	$\vdots$	

Tables of additive properties for these numbers are all of the same general pattern, but it is the smallest and simplest numbers which produce the greatest variety of useful additive properties. It is therefore interesting to find among the smaller numbers, not only ϕ and θ, but also the number 2, which plays a dominant part in commensurable systems of proportion, and the number $1 + \sqrt{3}$, which is sometimes found in incommensurable systems taking the place of ϕ or θ.

These four numbers, whose mathematical relationship is now apparent, are in fact at the basis of all the main historical systems of proportion. Hambidge's work suggests that they were already known to the Greeks, who regarded ϕ as the most important of them.[1] Unless some entirely new principle of architectural proportion is discovered, it seems unlikely that this judgment will be reversed.

[1] See p. 118 above.

BIBLIOGRAPHY

AUGUSTAN AGE

Vitruvius. *De architectura*. Editions: Barbaro, Venice, 1567; de Laet, Amsterdam, 1649; Granger, London, 1931. English translations: Newton, London, 1791; Wilkins (part only), London, 1812; Gwilt, London, 1826; Morgan, Cambridge, Mass., 1914; Granger, London, 1931.

FIFTEENTH, SIXTEENTH AND SEVENTEENTH CENTURIES

Alberti, Leon Battista. *De re aedificatoria*, Florence, 1485; translated by James Leoni as *Ten Books on Architecture*, London, 1726; new edition edited by Joseph Rykwert, London, 1955.

Cardan, Jerome. *De subtilitate*, Lyons, 1559.

Cennini, Cennino. *Il libro dell'arte*, edited and translated by D. V. Thompson, 2 volumes, New Haven, Conn., 1932–3.

Dürer, Albrecht. *De symmetria partium humanorum corporum*, Nuremberg, 1532; *The Literary Remains of A. Dürer*, edited by W. M. Conway, Cambridge, 1889.

Gaurico, Pomponio. *De sculptura*, 1504; published with de Laet's edition of Vitruvius, Amsterdam, 1649.

da Vinci, Leonardo. *The Literary Works of Leonardo da Vinci*, edited and translated by Dr J. P. Richter, second edition, Oxford, 1939; *Il Paragone: a Comparison of the Arts*, edited and translated by Irma A. Richter, Oxford, 1949; *Selections from the Notebooks of Leonardo da Vinci*, edited by Irma A. Richter, Oxford, 1952.

Lomazzo, G. P. *Trattato dell'arte della pittura, scultura ed architettura*, Milan, 1585; translated by Richard Haydock as *A Tracte containing the Artes of curious Paintinge, Carving and Building*, Oxford, 1598.

Palladio, Andrea. *I quattro libri dell'architettura*, Venice, 1570; translated by Isaac Ware as *The Four Books of Architecture*, London, 1738.

Perrault, Claude. *Ordonnances des cinq espèces de colonnes*, Paris, 1683; translated by John James as *A Treatise of the Five Orders of Columns in Architecture*, second edition, London, 1722.

Scamozzi, Vincente. *Idea dell'architettura universale*, Venice, 1615; translated into French by A. C. d'Aviler and Samuel Dury as *Œuvres d'architecture*, Leyden, 1713.

Shute, John. *The First and Chief Groundes of Architecture*, 1563; facsimile edition, London, 1912.

Vasari, Giorgio. *Le tre arti del disegno, cioè architettura, pittura, e scoltura*, included in the first edition of *Delle vite de' più eccellenti pittori, scultori, ed architettori*, Florence, 1550; translated by Louisa S. Maclehose and edited by Prof. G. Baldwin Brown as *Vasari on Technique*, London, 1907.

Wotton, Sir Henry. *Elements of Architecture*, 1624; fascimile edition, London, 1903.

Wren, Sir Christopher. 'Discourse on Architecture', printed in Lucy Phillimore's *Sir Christopher Wren*, London, 1881; 'Tracts', printed in James Elmes's *Memoirs of the Life and Works of Sir Christopher Wren*, London, 1823.

BIBLIOGRAPHY

EIGHTEENTH AND NINETEENTH CENTURIES (TO 1870)

Alison, Archibald. *Essays on the Nature and Principles of Taste*, 1790; second edition, 2 volumes, Edinburgh, 1811.

Barca, Alessandro. *Saggio sopra il bello di proporzione in architettura*, Bassano, 1806.

Berkeley, George. *Alciphron, or the Minute Philosopher*, 2 volumes, London, 1732.

Burke, Edmund. *A Philosophical Enquiry into the Origin of our Ideas of the Sublime and the Beautiful*, 1756; new edition, London, 1812.

Chambers, Sir William. *A Treatise on Civil Architecture*, London, 1759; edition edited by Joseph Gwilt and revised by W. H. Leeds, London, 1862.

Cockerell, C. R. *The Temples of Jupiter Panhellenius at Aegina and of Apollo Epicurius at Bassae, near Phigaleia in Arcadia*, containing W. W. Lloyd's 'Memoir of the systems of proportion employed in the design of the Doric temples at Phigaleia and Aegina', London, 1860.

Cresy, Edward. *Illustrations of Stone Church, Kent*, London, 1840; *Encyclopaedia of Civil Engineering* (1861), articles on proportion, which have been reprinted in the 1881 edition of Joseph Gwilt's *Encyclopaedia of Architecture*.

Gwilt, Joseph. *Rudiments of Architecture*, 1826; second edition, London, 1839.

Hay, D. R. *The Science of Beauty as developed in Nature and applied in Art*, Edinburgh, 1856.

Hogarth, William. *The Analysis of Beauty*, London, 1753; new edition edited by Joseph Burke, Oxford, 1955.

Hume, David. *Four Dissertations*, London, 1757.

Hutcheson, Francis. *An Inquiry into the Original of our Ideas of Beauty and Virtue*, 1725; fifth edition, London, 1753.

Kames, Lord. *Elements of Criticism*, 1762; eleventh edition, London, 1839.

Kerrich, T. 'Observations on the use of the mysterious figure, called the vesica piscis, in the architecture of the Middle Ages, and in Gothic architecture', *Archaeologia*, XIX (1821), pp. 353–68.

Knight, Richard Payne. *An Analytical Inquiry into the Principles of Taste*, 1805; third edition, London, 1816.

Legh, P. *Music of the Eye*, London, 1831.

Pennethorne, John. *The Elements and Mathematical Principles of the Greek Architects and Artists*, London, 1844.

Penrose, F. C. *An Investigation of the Principles of Athenian Architecture*, London, 1851.

Ruskin, John. *Modern Painters*, 1843–60; new edition in 6 volumes, London, 1898. *The Seven Lamps of Architecture*, London, 1849.

Scamozzi, O. B. *Le fabbriche e i disegni di Andrea Palladio*, 4 volumes, Vicenza, 1796.

Viollet-le-Duc, E. E. Article on 'Proportion' in volume VII of his *Dictionnaire raisonné de l'architecture française du XIe au XVIe siècle*, Paris, 1854–68.

LATE NINETEENTH AND TWENTIETH CENTURIES

(i) *Proportional theory*

Caskey, L. D. *Geometry of Greek Vases*, Boston, Mass., 1922.

Cook, Sir Theodore. *The Curves of Life*, London, 1914.

Le Corbusier, *Le Modulor*, Boulogne, 1950; translated by Peter de Francia and Anna Bostock as *The Modulor*, London, 1954; *Modulor 2*, Boulogne, 1954.

148

Edwards, A. Trystan. *The Things which are Seen*, 1921; second edition, London, 1947. *Style and Composition in Architecture*, 1926; second edition, 1944.

Ghyka, Matila. 'Frozen Music', article in *Horizon* (September 1943); 'Gothic canons of architecture', article in *Burlington Magazine* (March 1945); *The Geometry of Art and Life*, New York, 1946; 'Le Corbusier's Modulor', article in *Architectural Review* (February 1948); *A Practical Handbook of Geometrical Composition and Design*, London, 1952.

Hambidge, Jay. *Dynamic Symmetry: the Greek Vase*, New Haven, Conn., 1920; *The Parthenon and other Greek Temples: their Dynamic Symmetry*, New Haven, Conn., 1924; *The Elements of Dynamic Symmetry*, 1926, new edition, New Haven, Conn., 1948.

Lund, F. Macody. *Ad Quadratum*, 2 volumes, London, 1921.

Lutyens, Robert. *Sir Edwin Lutyens, an Appreciation in Perspective*, London, 1942.

Michel, Paul-Henri. *La Pensée de L. B. Alberti*, Paris, 1930.

Nobbs, Percy E. *Design: a Treatise on the Discovery of Form*, Oxford, 1937.

Roberts, A. Leonard. 'The achievement of proportion in architectural design', in *Architectural Design* (September 1948–February 1949).

Roberts, Harry. *R's Method of using Ordinary Set Squares*, London, 1927.

Robertson, Manning. 'The golden section or golden cut', in *R.I.B.A. Journal* (October 1948).

Robinson, John Beverly. *Principles of Architectural Composition*, New York, 1899; *Architectural Composition*, second edition, London and New York, 1914.

Rowe, Colin. 'Mathematics of the ideal villa', in *Architectural Review* (March 1947).

Teague, Walter Dorwin. *Design This Day*, London, 1946.

Wittkower, Rudolf. *Architectural Principles in the Age of Humanism*, London, 1949; second edition, 1952.

Wölfflin, Heinrich. *Zur Lehre von den Proportionen*, 1889, reprinted in *Kleine Schriften*, Basle, 1946.

(ii) *Aesthetics*

Bosanquet, Bernard. *History of Aesthetic*, London, 1892.

Carritt, E. F. *Philosophies of Beauty*, Oxford, 1931.

Collingwood, R. G. *The Principles of Art*, Oxford, 1938.

Gilbert, Katherine Everett and Helmut Kuhn. *A History of Esthetics*, New York, 1939.

Katz, D. and H. S. Langfeld. Article on 'Aesthetics, experimental', in the 1947 edition of the *Encyclopaedia Britannica*.

Osborne, H. *Theory of Beauty: an Introduction to Aesthetics*, London, 1952.

(iii) *Mathematics*

Cantor, Moritz. *Vorlesungen über Geschichte der Mathematik*, 3 volumes, second edition, Leipzig, 1894–1901.

Danzig, Tobias. *Number, the Language of Science*, second British edition, London, 1940.

Dickson, L. E. *History of the Theory of Numbers*, 3 volumes, Washington, 1919–23.

Euclid, *The Thirteen Books of Euclid's Elements*, translated with commentary by Sir T. L. Heath, 3 volumes, Cambridge, 1908; second edition, 1926.

Heath, Sir T. L. *A History of Greek Mathematics*, 2 volumes, Oxford, 1921.

Lucas, E. 'Théorie des fonctions numériques simplement périodiques', *American Journal of Mathematics*, 1 (1878), pp. 184 ff. and 289 ff.

Michel, Paul-Henri. *De Pythagore à Euclide, contribution à l'histoire des mathématiques préeuclidiennes*, Paris, 1950.

BIBLIOGRAPHY

Nicomachus of Gerasa, *Introductio arithmetica*; translated into English as *Introduction to Arithmetic* by M. L. d'Ooge, with studies in Greek arithmetic by F. E. Robbins and L. C. Karpinski, London and New York, 1926.

Thompson, Sir D'Arcy Wentworth. 'Excess and defect: or the little more and the little less', *Mind*, XXXVIII (1929), pp. 43 ff.

(iv) *Metrology*

Berriman, A. E. *Historical Metrology*, London, 1953.

Petrie, Sir W. M. Flinders. Article on 'Measures and weights, ancient', in the 1947 edition of the *Encyclopaedia Britannica*.

(v) *Music*

Jeans, Sir James. *Science and Music*, Cambridge, 1937.

Wood, A. *The Physical Basis of Music*, Cambridge, 1913.

INDEX

INDEX